Teach Yourself
Excel 2000
VISUALLY™
Student Workbook

Teach Yourself Excel 2000 VISUALLY™
Student Workbook

Sandra Cable
Sherry Kinkoph

IDG Books Worldwide, Inc.
An International Data Group Company
Foster City, CA • Chicago, IL • Indianapolis, IN • New York, NY

Teach Yourself Excel 2000 VISUALLY™
Student Workbook

Published by
IDG Books Worldwide, Inc.
An International Data Group Company
919 E. Hillsdale Blvd., Suite 400
Foster City, CA 94404
www.idgbooks.com

Copyright © 2000 IDG Books Worldwide, Inc.

Artwork copyright (c)1999 maranGraphics, Inc.

All rights reserved. No part of this book, including interior design, cover design, and icons, may be reproduced or transmitted in any form, by any means (electronic, photocopying, recording, or otherwise) without the prior written permission of the publisher.

Printed in the United States of America

ISBN 0-7645-3438-6

10 9 8 7 6 5 4 3 2 1

1B/ST/RR/ZZ/IN

Distributed in the United States by IDG Books Worldwide, Inc.

Distributed by CDG Books Canada Inc. for Canada; by Transworld Publishers Limited in the United Kingdom; by IDG Norge Books for Norway; by IDG Sweden Books for Sweden; by IDG Books Australia Publishing Corporation Pty. Ltd. for Australia and New Zealand; by TransQuest Publishers Pte Ltd. for Singapore, Malaysia, Thailand, Indonesia, and Hong Kong; by Gotop Information Inc. for Taiwan; by ICG Muse, Inc. for Japan; by Intersoft for South Africa; by Eyrolles for France; by International Thomson Publishing for Germany, Austria and Switzerland; by Distribuidora Cuspide for Argentina; by LR International for Brazil; by Galileo Libros for Chile; by Ediciones ZETA S.C.R. Ltda. for Peru; by WS Computer Publishing Corporation, Inc., for the Philippines; by Contemporanea de Ediciones for Venezuela; by Express Computer Distributors for the Caribbean and West Indies; by Micronesia Media Distributor, Inc. for Micronesia; by Chips Computadoras S.A. de C.V. for Mexico; by Editorial Norma de Panama S.A. for Panama; by American Bookshops for Finland.

For general information on IDG Books Worldwide's books in the U.S., please call our Consumer Customer Service department at 800-762-2974. For reseller information, including discounts and premium sales, please call our Reseller Customer Service department at 800-434-3422.

For information on where to purchase IDG Books Worldwide's books outside the U.S., please contact our International Sales department at 317-596-5530 or fax 317-596-5692.

For consumer information on foreign language translations, please contact our Customer Service department at 1-800-434-3422, fax 317-596-5692, or e-mail rights@idgbooks.com.

For information on licensing foreign or domestic rights, please phone +1-650-655-3109.

For sales inquiries and special prices for bulk quantities, please contact our Sales department at 650-655-3200 or write to the address above.

For information on using IDG Books Worldwide's books in the classroom or for ordering examination copies, please contact our Educational Sales department at 800-434-2086 or fax 317-596-5499.

For press review copies, author interviews, or other publicity information, please contact our Public Relations department at 650-655-3000 or fax 650-655-3299.

For authorization to photocopy items for corporate, personal, or educational use, please contact Copyright Clearance Center, 222 Rosewood Drive, Danvers, MA 01923, or fax 978-750-4470.

> **LIMIT OF LIABILITY/DISCLAIMER OF WARRANTY: THE PUBLISHER AND AUTHOR HAVE USED THEIR BEST EFFORTS IN PREPARING THIS BOOK. THE PUBLISHER AND AUTHOR MAKE NO REPRESENTATIONS OR WARRANTIES WITH RESPECT TO THE ACCURACY OR COMPLETENESS OF THE CONTENTS OF THIS BOOK AND SPECIFICALLY DISCLAIM ANY IMPLIED WARRANTIES OF MERCHANTABILITY OR FITNESS FOR A PARTICULAR PURPOSE. THERE ARE NO WARRANTIES WHICH EXTEND BEYOND THE DESCRIPTIONS CONTAINED IN THIS PARAGRAPH. NO WARRANTY MAY BE CREATED OR EXTENDED BY SALES REPRESENTATIVES OR WRITTEN SALES MATERIALS. THE ACCURACY AND COMPLETENESS OF THE INFORMATION PROVIDED HEREIN AND THE OPINIONS STATED HEREIN ARE NOT GUARANTEED OR WARRANTED TO PRODUCE ANY PARTICULAR RESULTS, AND THE ADVICE AND STRATEGIES CONTAINED HEREIN MAY NOT BE SUITABLE FOR EVERY INDIVIDUAL. NEITHER THE PUBLISHER NOR AUTHOR SHALL BE LIABLE FOR ANY LOSS OF PROFIT OR ANY OTHER COMMERCIAL DAMAGES, INCLUDING BUT NOT LIMITED TO SPECIAL, INCIDENTAL, CONSEQUENTIAL, OR OTHER DAMAGES.**

Trademarks: All brand names and product names used in this book are trade names, service marks, trademarks, or registered trademarks of their respective owners. IDG Books Worldwide is not associated with any product or vendor mentioned in this book.

IDG BOOKS WORLDWIDE® is a registered trademark under exclusive license to IDG Books Worldwide, Inc., from International Data Group, Inc.

ABOUT IDG BOOKS WORLDWIDE

Welcome to the world of IDG Books Worldwide.

IDG Books Worldwide, Inc., is a subsidiary of International Data Group, the world's largest publisher of computer-related information and the leading global provider of information services on information technology. IDG was founded more than 30 years ago by Patrick J. McGovern and now employs more than 9,000 people worldwide. IDG publishes more than 290 computer publications in over 75 countries. More than 90 million people read one or more IDG publications each month.

Launched in 1990, IDG Books Worldwide is today the #1 publisher of best-selling computer books in the United States. We are proud to have received eight awards from the Computer Press Association in recognition of editorial excellence and three from Computer Currents' First Annual Readers' Choice Awards. Our best-selling ...*For Dummies*® series has more than 50 million copies in print with translations in 31 languages. IDG Books Worldwide, through a joint venture with IDG's Hi-Tech Beijing, became the first U.S. publisher to publish a computer book in the People's Republic of China. In record time, IDG Books Worldwide has become the first choice for millions of readers around the world who want to learn how to better manage their businesses.

Our mission is simple: Every one of our books is designed to bring extra value and skill-building instructions to the reader. Our books are written by experts who understand and care about our readers. The knowledge base of our editorial staff comes from years of experience in publishing, education, and journalism — experience we use to produce books to carry us into the new millennium. In short, we care about books, so we attract the best people. We devote special attention to details such as audience, interior design, use of icons, and illustrations. And because we use an efficient process of authoring, editing, and desktop publishing our books electronically, we can spend more time ensuring superior content and less time on the technicalities of making books.

You can count on our commitment to deliver high-quality books at competitive prices on topics you want to read about. At IDG Books Worldwide, we continue in the IDG tradition of delivering quality for more than 30 years. You'll find no better book on a subject than one from IDG Books Worldwide.

John Kilcullen
Chairman and CEO
IDG Books Worldwide, Inc.

Steven Berkowitz
President and Publisher
IDG Books Worldwide, Inc.

Eighth Annual Computer Press Awards ≥1992

Ninth Annual Computer Press Awards ≥1993

Tenth Annual Computer Press Awards ≥1994

Eleventh Annual Computer Press Awards ≥1995

IDG is the world's leading IT media, research and exposition company. Founded in 1964, IDG had 1997 revenues of $2.05 billion and has more than 9,000 employees worldwide. IDG offers the widest range of media options that reach IT buyers in 75 countries representing 95% of worldwide IT spending. IDG's diverse product and services portfolio spans six key areas including print publishing, online publishing, expositions and conferences, market research, education and training, and global marketing services. More than 90 million people read one or more of IDG's 290 magazines and newspapers, including IDG's leading global brands — Computerworld, PC World, Network World, Macworld and the Channel World family of publications. IDG Books Worldwide is one of the fastest-growing computer book publishers in the world, with more than 700 titles in 36 languages. The "...For Dummies®" series alone has more than 50 million copies in print. IDG offers online users the largest network of technology-specific Web sites around the world through IDG.net (http://www.idg.net), which comprises more than 225 targeted Web sites in 55 countries worldwide. International Data Corporation (IDC) is the world's largest provider of information technology data, analysis and consulting, with research centers in over 41 countries and more than 400 research analysts worldwide. IDG World Expo is a leading producer of more than 168 globally branded conferences and expositions in 35 countries including E3 (Electronic Entertainment Expo), Macworld Expo, ComNet, Windows World Expo, ICE (Internet Commerce Expo), Agenda, DEMO, and Spotlight. IDG's training subsidiary, ExecuTrain, is the world's largest computer training company, with more than 230 locations worldwide and 785 training courses. IDG Marketing Services helps industry-leading IT companies build international brand recognition by developing global integrated marketing programs via IDG's print, online and exposition products worldwide. Further information about the company can be found at www.idg.com.   1/24/99

Credits

Senior Editor, Freelance
Constance Carlisle

Project Editor
Anne Owen

Acquisitions Editor
Martine Edwards

Acquisitions Associate Project Coordinator
Lindsay Sandman

Media Development Manager
Heather Dismore

Associate Media Development Editor
Megan Decraene

Associate Permissions Editor
Carmen Kirikorian

Technical Reviewer
Marita Ellixson

Project Coordinator
Cindy L. Phipps

Layout and Graphics
Janet Seib, Michael Sullivan,
Dan Whetstine, Erin Zeltner

Proofreaders
Betty Kish, Rebecca Senninger

Special Help
Christine Berman, Barry Childs-Helton
James Russell

About the Authors

Sandra Cable, MBA, is an author and professional educator who has served as a Microsoft Office training consultant for Southwest Airlines, Memorex/Telex Corporation, Wright State University, and numerous other educational institutions. She is currently working toward her Doctorate in Educational Administration at Texas A&M University.

Sherry Kinkoph has authored over 40 computer books over the past seven years covering a variety of topics, including Microsoft Office, Quicken, Microsoft Works, and the Internet. A native of the Midwest, Sherry currently resides in Fishers, Indiana, and continues to teach users around the world how to make sense of computers and the software that makes them so much fun.

General and Administrative

IDG Books Worldwide, Inc.: John Kilcullen, CEO; Steven Berkowitz, President and Publisher

IDG Books Technology Publishing Group: Richard Swadley, Senior Vice President and Publisher; Walter Bruce III, Vice President and Associate Publisher; Joseph Wikert, Associate Publisher; Mary Bednarek, Branded Product Development Director; Mary Corder, Editorial Director; Barry Pruett, Publishing Manager; Michelle Baxter, Publishing Manager

IDG Books Consumer Publishing Group: Roland Elgey, Senior Vice President and Publisher; Kathleen A. Welton, Vice President and Publisher; Kevin Thornton, Acquisitions Manager; Kristin A. Cocks, Editorial Director

IDG Books Internet Publishing Group: Brenda McLaughlin, Senior Vice President and Publisher; Diane Graves Steele, Vice President and Associate Publisher; Sofia Marchant, Online Marketing Manager

IDG Books Production for Dummies Press: Debbie Stailey, Associate Director of Production; Cindy L. Phipps, Manager of Project Coordination, Production Proofreading, and Indexing; Tony Augsburger, Manager of Prepress, Reprints, and Systems; Laura Carpenter, Production Control Manager; Shelley Lea, Supervisor of Graphics and Design; Debbie J. Gates, Production Systems Specialist; Robert Springer, Supervisor of Proofreading; Kathie Schutte, Production Supervisor

Dummies Packaging and Book Design: Patty Page, Manager, Promotions Marketing

The publisher would like to give special thanks to Patrick J. McGovern,
without whom this book would not have been possible.

Table of Contents

Overview 1
   How to Use This Workbook *1*
   About the Textbook *1*
   Before You Begin *2*
   Classroom Suggestions *2*

Module 1: Getting Started with Excel 2000 5
Chapter Coverage 5
Tests and Projects Included 5
Materials and Resources 5
Module 1 Objectives 6
Exercises and Projects 7
   Module 1 Multiple Choice Questions *7*
   Module 1 Fill-in-the-Blank Questions ... *11*
   Module 1 Challenge Questions *13*
   Project #1: Your First Workbook *15*
   Project #2: Opening an Existing Workbook *17*
   Project #3: Switching Between Open Workbooks ... *19*

Module 2: Editing Worksheets and Using Formulas 21
Chapter Coverage 21
Tests and Projects Included 21
Materials and Resources 21
Module 2 Objectives 22
Exercises and Projects 23
   Module 2 Multiple Choice Questions *23*
   Module 2 Fill-in-the-Blank Questions .. *27*

   Module 2 Challenge Questions *29*
   Project #1: Applying the AutoSum Function *31*
   Project #2: Creating Formulas and Linking Data .. *33*
   Project #3: Using and Displaying Formulas *35*
   Taking It Even Further *36*

Module 3: Viewing and Formatting Workbooks .37
Chapter Coverage 37
Tests and Projects Included 37
Materials and Resources 37
Module 3 Objectives 38
Exercises and Projects 39
   Module 3 Multiple Choice Questions *39*
   Module 3 Fill-in-the-Blank Questions .. *43*
   Module 3 Challenge Questions *45*
   Project #1: Changing the Screen Display *47*
   Project #2: Formatting Data *49*
   Taking It Even Further *50*
   Project #3: Centering Data Across Columns ... *51*

Module 4: Printing and Using Multiple Worksheets 53
Chapter Coverage 53
Tests and Projects Included 53
Materials and Resources 53
Module 4 Objectives 54

Student Workbook
Teach Yourself Excel 2000 VISUALLY

Exercises and Projects 55
   Module 4 Multiple Choice Questions *55*
   Module 4 Fill-in-the-Blank Questions *59*
   Module 4 Challenge Questions *61*
   Project #1: Changing Print Options *63*
   Project #2: Using Formulas Across Worksheets . . . *65*
   Taking It Even Further *66*

Module 5: Working with Charts and Graphics . . 67
Chapter Coverage 67
Tests and Projects Included 67
Materials and Resources 67
Module 5 Objectives 68
Exercises and Projects 69
   Module 5 Multiple Choice Questions *69*
   Module 5 Fill-in-the-Blank Questions *73*
   Module 5 Challenge Questions *75*
   Project #1: Create a Chart *77*
   Project #2: Adding Graphics *79*
   Taking It Even Further *80*

Module 6: Working with Macros, Lists, and Hyperlinks 81
Chapter Coverage 81
Tests and Projects Included 81
Materials and Resources 81
Module 6 Objectives 82
Exercises and Projects 83
   Module 6 Multiple Choice Questions *83*
   Module 6 Fill-in-the-Blank Questions *87*
   Module 6 Challenge Questions *89*
   Project #1: Creating a Macro *91*
   Project #2: Applying a Custom AutoFilter *93*
   Taking It Even Further *94*

Glossary 95

Overview

Welcome to the Student Workbook for *Teach Yourself Excel 2000 VISUALLY*.

This workbook is designed for in-class or self-paced learning. Using the textbook as the foundation, it will help guide you from basic skills through more advanced features and functions of Microsoft Excel 2000.

The exercises and projects included are appropriate for new Excel 2000 users, as well as for users with intermediate or more advanced knowledge.

This course may include visual aids in a PowerPoint format. These visual aids coincide with the flow of the textbook, as well as the modules in this workbook. They are designed for either formal classroom discussion or self-study settings.

How to Use This Workbook

This workbook is comprised of six modules, each designed to build skills that will lead into the next. To ensure a successful learning experience, follow the modules and their respective chapters in the textbook in order.

Each module in this workbook includes the following:

- A list of objectives
- Exercises in multiple choice, fill-in-the-blanks, and challenge formats, designed to reinforce your knowledge and skills as you complete the module
- Hands-on projects, with easy-to-follow directions

Use the exam at the back of the book to test your overall understanding of Excel and the topics covered in the course.

This workbook also includes a comprehensive glossary of terms you will learn as you complete the course.

About the Textbook

Teach Yourself Excel 2000 VISUALLY was written to introduce new users to Excel 2000, as well as build on any previously learned skills, using step-by-step illustrated tasks. The book is laid out logically, from basic skills through more advanced topics. Excel 2000 topics covered in this book include:

- Opening and saving workbooks
- Working with cells and data
- Using formulas and functions
- Changing your display and formatting worksheets

- Working with multiple worksheets
- Using charts and graphics
- Excel 2000 and the Internet

The textbook also reviews basic Windows skills to prepare you for working with Excel 2000.

Before You Begin

Prior to beginning this unit, you should possess a basic understanding of operating a computer in the Windows environment.

You should have exclusive access to a PC with Windows 95 or 98 and Excel 2000 installed and running at the beginning of each class to allow quick access.

A copy of *Teach Yourself Excel 2000 VISUALLY* and the student workbook should be in your possession during the course. You should also have available notepaper and pens or pencils.

Classroom Suggestions

You should first review the appropriate chapters before beginning each module. Be involved during classroom presentation and discussion of the lessons. After the presentations and discussions, your instructor will administer exercises and projects related to the subject matter.

Teach Yourself
Excel 2000
VISUALLY™
Student Workbook

Module 1: Getting Started with Excel 2000
Includes textbook Chapters 1 & 2

Module 2: Editing Worksheets and Using Formulas
Includes textbook Chapters 3 & 4

Module 3: Viewing and Formatting Workbooks
Includes textbook Chapters 5 & 6

Module 4: Printing and Using Multiple Worksheets
Includes textbook Chapters 7 & 8

Module 5: Working with Charts and Graphics
Includes textbook Chapters 9 & 10

Module 6: Macros, Lists, and Hyperlinks
Includes textbook Chapters 11, 12 & 13

Module 1: Getting Started with Excel 2000

Chapter Coverage

CHAPTER 1 GETTING STARTED
CHAPTER 2 SAVE AND OPEN YOUR WORKBOOKS

Tests and Projects Included

Test Title	Chapter Reference
Module 1 Multiple Choice	1 through 2
Module 1 Fill-in-the-Blank	1 through 2
Module 1 Challenge Questions	1 through 2

Project Title	Chapter Reference
Project 1 Your First Workbook	1 and 2
Project 2 Opening an Existing Workbook	1 and 2
Project 3 Switching Between Open Workbooks	1 and 2

Materials and Resources

The materials and resources required for successfully completing this module include:

- A computer running Microsoft Excel 2000 and Microsoft PowerPoint
- Starter files for the projects
- A color monitor
- A printer, connected to the computer, loaded with paper, online, and ready to print
- At least 30 megabytes of available hard drive space

Student Workbook
Teach Yourself Excel 2000 VISUALLY

Module 1 Objectives

Upon completion of this module, you will be competent in the following areas:

Skill	Chapter
Using the Mouse	Chapter 1
Starting Excel 2000	Chapter 1
Utilizing the Excel Screen	Chapter 1
Understanding the Active Cell	Chapter 1
Entering Data	Chapter 1
Selecting Cells	Chapter 1
Completing a Series	Chapter 1
Moving Through a Workbook	Chapter 1
Getting Help	Chapter 1
Saving a Workbook	Chapter 2
Protecting a Workbook	Chapter 2
Creating a New Workbook	Chapter 2
Switching Between Workbooks	Chapter 2
Viewing All Open Workbooks	Chapter 2
Closing a Workbook	Chapter 2
Exiting Excel	Chapter 2
Opening Workbooks	Chapter 2
Finding a Workbook	Chapter 2

Exercises and Projects

Module 1 Multiple Choice Questions
Please circle the letter in front of the correct response for each question.

1. In Microsoft Excel, how can you start a new workbook?
   a. You can use the File menu, and then select the New command
   b. You can click the New button
   c. You can press CTRL+N
   d. All of the above

2. To view an expanded menu, you must:
   a. Open the menu, wait a few moments, and the full menu will display
   b. Click anywhere outside the menu
   c. Click the downward-pointing arrows at the bottom of the menu
   d. Both a and c

3. To find out the name of a toolbar button:
   a. Open the Customize dialog box
   b. Hover your mouse pointer over the button to display a ScreenTip with the button's name
   c. Click the button
   d. None of the above

4. How can you determine which cell is the active cell?
   a. The active cell has a thick border
   b. The reference for the active cell appears in the Name box to the left of the Formula bar
   c. You can click the Edit menu, and then select View to display the active cell
   d. Both a and b

5. After creating a workbook, what action should you take first to keep the workbook for future use?
   a. You should open the workbook
   b. You should close the workbook
   c. You should save the workbook
   d. You should copy the workbook

Student Workbook
Teach Yourself Excel 2000 VISUALLY

6. When you open the File menu and select the Save As command, you can:
   a. Save the workbook in a format other than Excel 2000's format
   b. Save the workbook in a folder other than the My Documents folder
   c. Save the workbook with a different file name than it was originally named
   d. All of the above

7. When switching between open workbooks:
   a. You can click the Window menu, and then click the workbook name at the bottom of this menu
   b. You can click the workbook button you want to use on the Windows Taskbar at the bottom of the window
   c. You can press CTRL+F6
   d. All of the above

8. How do you select more than one cell in a worksheet?
   a. Click the first cell in the group, and then drag over the adjacent cells to highlight your selection
   b. You can select only one cell at a time in Excel 2000
   c. Hold down the Alt key while clicking on the cells you want to select
   d. Click anywhere in a row or column

9. If you close a workbook in Excel, what happens to that workbook?
   a. The workbook is removed from your screen
   b. The workbook is removed from your screen and deleted from your hard drive
   c. The workbook is replaced with a new workbook
   d. The workbook is saved automatically and then removed from the screen

10. Why would it be beneficial to view multiple workbooks in Excel?
    a. Viewing multiple workbooks allows more of the active workbook to display on your screen
    b. Viewing multiple workbooks changes how the active workbook will be printed
    c. Viewing multiple workbooks lets you view and compare data between workbooks
    d. All of the above

MODULE 1
EXERCISES AND PROJECTS

11. To display the Office Assistant:
    a. Click the Microsoft Excel Help button on the Standard toolbar
    b. Open the Help menu and select Microsoft Excel Help
    c. Press F1 on the keyboard
    d. All of the above

12. What action must you take to view additional Help tabs in the Help window?
    a. Click the Forward button
    b. Click the Close button
    c. Click the Show button
    b. None of the above

13. What is the Formula Bar used for in Excel?
    a. Creating formulas and entering data within a cell and allowing changes to this data
    b. Displaying and changing margins
    c. Displaying formula totals
    d. Moving and copying data

14. Excel's AutoFill feature can save you time by helping you complete what kind of series?
    a. Text series, such as the months of the year
    b. Number series, such as 5, 10, 15, 20
    c. Text label series, such as Qtr1, Qtr2, Qtr3
    d. All of the above

15. Using a password when saving a workbook allows you to protect the workbook from what?
    a. You can protect the workbook from unauthorized viewing
    b. You can protect the workbook from unauthorized changes
    c. You can protect the workbook from being displayed in the file list
    d. Both a and b

16. What is Excel's vertical scroll bar used for?
    a. The scroll bar can move the insertion point to different locations in the workbook
    b. The scroll bar moves the display up or down in the workbook when the workbook is longer than one screen can display
    c. Both a and b
    d. Neither a nor b

17. If you use a password for opening a workbook, how can you display the workbook if you forget the password?
    a. You can't open the workbook without the password
    b. You can open the file by clicking Cancel in the Password dialog box
    c. You can copy the workbook, and the copy will not require a password
    d. None of the above

18. When typing into a worksheet, should you use the Enter key on the keyboard?
    a. You should use the Enter key when you want to select the cell below the active cell
    b. You should never use the Enter key in Excel
    c. You should use the Enter key when you want to move to the right of the active cell
    d. All of the above

19. How do you hide the Office Assistant so it no longer appears onscreen?
    a. Right-click the Office Assistant and select Hide from the pop-up menu that appears
    b. Open the Help menu and choose Hide the Office Assistant
    c. Open the Help menu and choose Microsoft Excel Help
    d. Both a and b

20. To get Excel to complete a series, you will first need to place your mouse pointer:
    a. Over the bottom-right corner of the selected cell(s)
    b. Over the Fill Handle, the bottom-left corner of the selected cell(s)
    c. Across the top of the selected cell(s)
    d. None of the above

Module 1
Exercises and Projects

WORD LIST

Active Cell
Arrange
Cell Reference
Cells
Fill Handle
Formula Bar
Office Assistant
Password
Row Header
Save
Scroll Bar
Title Bar
Workbooks
Worksheet
Worksheet Tab

Module 1 Fill-in-the-Blank Questions
Select the appropriate word from the list to fill in the blanks:

1. Microsoft Excel can be used to edit, format, and print _____.

2. The _____ is the cell currently selected in the worksheet and surrounded by a bold line.

3. After creating a workbook in Excel, you should _____ it for future use.

4. The _____ allows you to enter plain text questions to search for help in using Excel.

5. The _____ displays the cell reference and an area for building and editing formulas and data.

6. To select an entire row in a worksheet, click the _____.

7. To complete a series, simply place your mouse pointer over the _____ of the selected cell(s) and drag.

8. The Name box at the far left end of the Formula Bar shows the _____ of the active cell.

9. To move the display of a workbook up or down, you can use Excel's _____.

10. You use a _____ to protect a workbook.

11. A _____ is a one-spreadsheet page in a workbook.

12. You would choose the _____ option in the Window menu if you wanted to view several opened workbooks at the same time.

13. The name of the workbook appears at the _____ at the top of the screen.

14. To move to another worksheet within the same workbook, you need to click the _____ at the bottom of the screen.

15. An Excel worksheet consists of rows, columns, and _____.

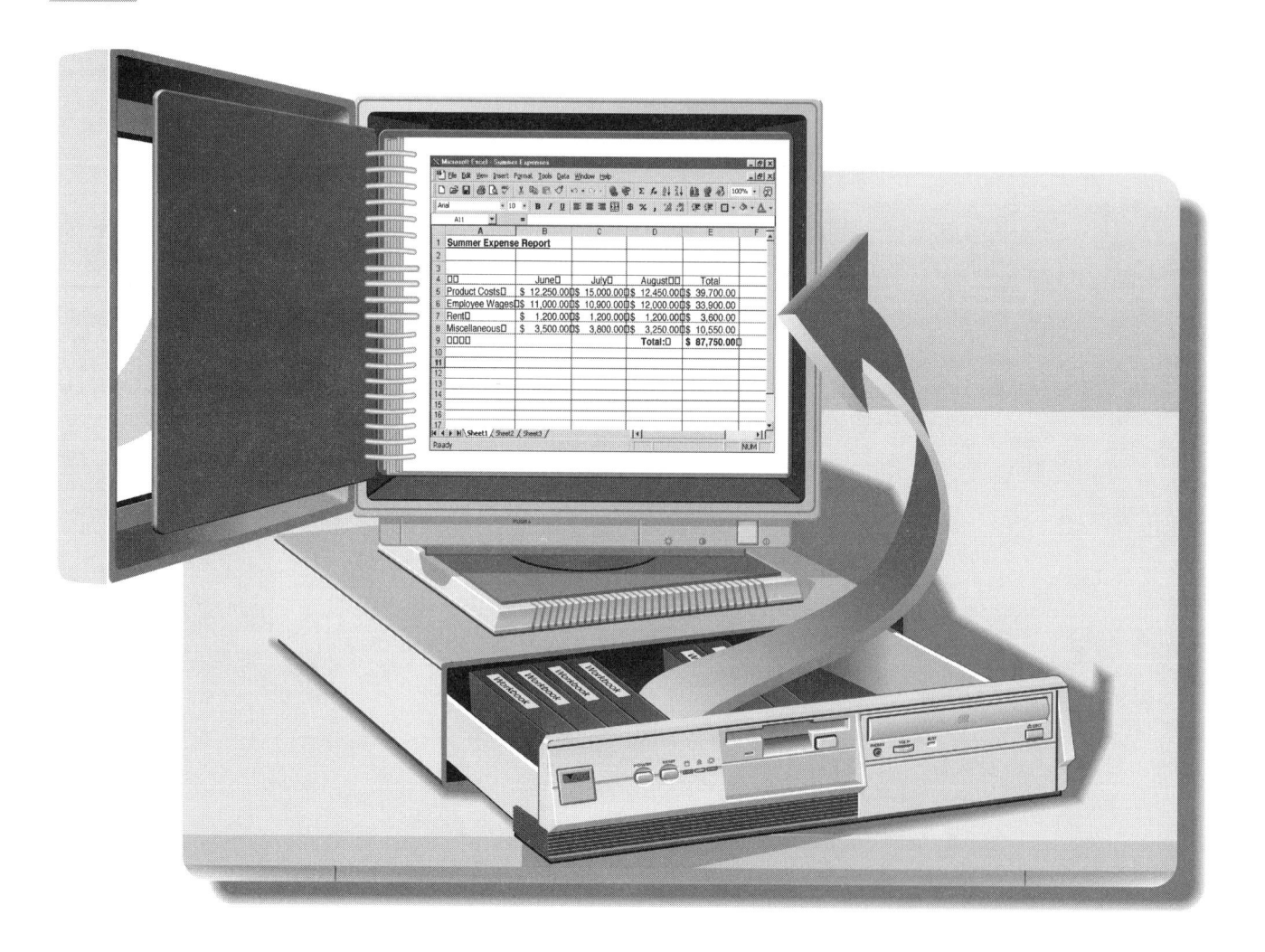

Student Workbook
Teach Yourself Excel 2000 VISUALLY

Module 1 Challenge Questions

Please use a sentence or a short paragraph to answer the following questions:

1. Describe, in order, how you can protect a workbook from unauthorized use.

2. After opening the Office Assistant, how can you find help for using a feature in Excel? (include an example)

3. Describe the steps for viewing multiple workbooks.

4. Why would you want to save a workbook in a format other than Excel Workbook format?

5. While editing a workbook, you click File in the menu bar, and then Exit. What action does Excel take?

6. What types of data can you enter into an Excel worksheet?

Student Workbook
Teach Yourself Excel 2000 VISUALLY

7. Describe the different methods for switching between open workbooks.

8. In the Help window, which tab contains an alphabetical list of all the help topics available?

9. How can you create a duplicate of a workbook in Excel?

10. How many workbook names does Excel keep track of at the bottom of the File menu?

MODULE 1
EXERCISES AND PROJECTS

Project #1: Your First Workbook

This first project teaches you how to create a brand new workbook, enter data into a worksheet, print the worksheet, and then save the file. In addition, you will use Excel's AutoFill feature to complete a series of data.

Scenario:

As Chief Financial Officer for The Pet Mart chain, you need to provide a semiannual budget report to the company's president. Shown here is the budget information. You will enter this data into a worksheet and save the workbook as BUDGET.XLS.

Student Name

Teach Yourself Excel 2000 VISUALLY

Module 1 Project 1

The Pet Mart
Semi-Annual Budget

	January	February	March	April	May	June
Department 1	53.5	57.35	61.2	65.05	68.9	72.75
Department 2	65	68.25	71.5	74.75	78	81.25
Department 3	99	107.3	115.6	123.9	132.2	140.5
Department 4	45.5	42.25	39	35.75	32.5	29.25
Department 5	45	46.75	48.5	50.25	52	53.75
Department 6	67	69.25	71.5	73.75	76	78.25

What you'll need:

A computer running Windows 95 or 98 and Microsoft Excel 2000
A printer, connected to the computer, with paper, online, and ready to print

What to do:

1. **Start Excel 2000 and a new workbook file**
   a. Click the Start button on the Windows Taskbar, move the mouse pointer to Programs, and then click Microsoft Excel.
   b. Excel opens, and a new, blank workbook appears automatically.

2. **Begin entering text**
   a. Type your name in cell A1 and press Enter twice on the keyboard.
   b. Type **Teach Yourself Excel 2000 VISUALLY** in cell A3 and press Enter twice on the keyboard.
   c. Type **Module 1 Project 1** in cell A5.

Student Workbook
Teach Yourself Excel 2000 VISUALLY

3. Create a data series with AutoFill
   a. Click inside cell B10 and type **January**.
   b. Use AutoFill to fill the data series of months (February through June) through cell G10.
   c. Click inside cell A11 and type **Department 1**.
   d. Use AutoFill to fill the data series of department titles (Department 2 through Department 6) through cell A16.

4. Enter budget data
   a. Click inside cell B11 and type **53.5**.
   b. Enter the remaining budget data shown in the figure at the beginning of this project.

5. Save the workbook
   a. Open the File menu and select Save As.
   b. When the Save As dialog box opens, type **BUDGET** in the File name box and then press Enter to save the workbook.

6. Print the workbook
   a. Make sure your printer is turned on, with paper loaded in the appropriate tray.
   b. Open the File menu and select Print.
   c. When the Print dialog box opens, click the OK button to print the workbook.

7. Close Excel
   a. Open the File menu and choose Exit.

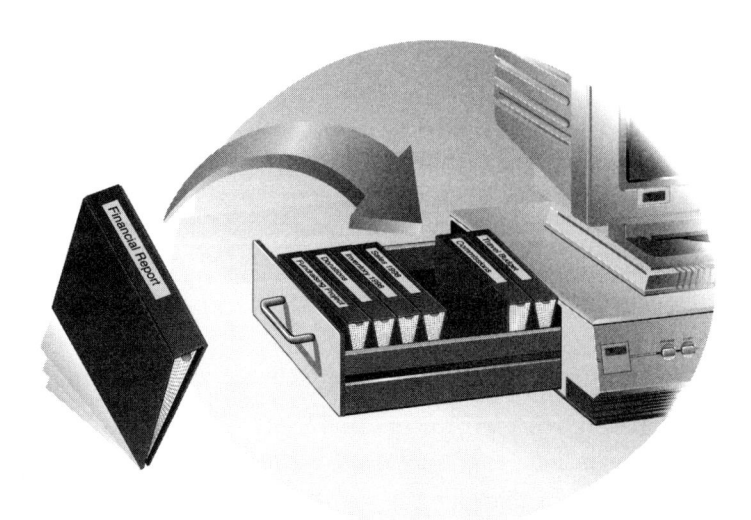

Project #2: Opening an Existing Workbook

This project concentrates on a previously saved workbook file, called PASSWORD.XLS. Using this file, you will make some changes to the data, assign a password to the file, and print the worksheet.

Scenario:

You are the Inventory Manager for The Computer Parts Store. The current inventory information is located in the PASSWORD.XLS workbook. You've just received two new items from the manufacturer that need to be added to the inventory data. Use the following information to make your modifications to the workbook:

In cell A11 change the Part Number: 123456
In cell B11 change the Cost: $157.98
In cell C11 change the Description: 486 Processor – Special Order Only
In cell B16 change the Part Number: 654321
In cell C16 change the Cost: $3317.66
In cell D16 change the Description: Carrier Assembly

What to do:

1. **Open Excel 2000 and open PASSWORD.XLS**
   a. Start Excel.
   b. Display the File menu and select Open, and then locate and open the PASSWORD.XLS workbook.

2. **Enter new data**
   a. In cell A1 type your name and press Enter twice.
   b. Type **Teach Yourself Excel 2000 VISUALLY** and press Enter twice.
   c. Type **Module 1 Project 2**.

3. **Edit the existing data**
   a. Edit the changes to the data as listed at the beginning of this project by clicking in the appropriate cell, entering the changes, and pressing Enter.

4. **Password protect the workbook**
   a. Open the File menu and choose Save As.
   b. Click the Tools button in the Save As dialog box toolbar to display a drop-down menu of options, and then select General Options.
   c. Click inside the Password to Modify field and enter the password **PASSWORD**.
   d. Click the OK button.
   e. Retype the password to confirm. Then click OK.

5. Save the workbook

a. The Save As dialog box remains onscreen. Type **PASSWORD2** and then press Enter to save the workbook.

6. Print the workbook

a. Make sure your printer is turned on, with paper loaded in the appropriate tray.
b. Click the Print button on the Standard toolbar.

7. Close the workbook

a. Open the File menu and select Close.

8. Open the workbook using the password

a. Click the Open button on the Standard toolbar, and then double-click the PASSWORD2.XLS workbook file.
b. The Password dialog box appears onscreen. Enter the password you assigned in step 4, and then press Enter.

9. Close the workbook and exit Excel

a. Click the Excel program window's Close button (the button with an X in the upper-right corner of the Excel window).

Student Name
Teach Yourself Excel 2000 VISUALLY
Module 1 Project 2

The Computer Parts Store
Product List

Part Number	Cost	Description
123456	$ 157.98	486 Processor - Special Order Only
345124	$ 298.34	586 Processor
355760	$ 427.76	686 Processor
366396	$ 557.18	786 Processor
377032	$ 686.60	886 Processor
654321	$ 3,317.66	Carrier Assembly

Project #3: Switching Between Open Workbooks

The final project for this module lets you practice viewing multiple workbooks onscreen at the same time and switching between open workbooks.

Scenario:

You are the accountant for both The Pet Mart and The Computer Parts Store. You need to compare data between workbooks.

What to do:

1. **Open the BUDGET.XLS, PASSWORD.XLS, and PASSWORD2.XLS files**
   a. Start Excel.
   b. Click the Open button on the Standard toolbar to display the Open dialog box.
   c. Locate the BUDGET.XLS file you created in Project 1, and then double-click the file name to open the workbook.
   d. Click the Open button on the Standard toolbar again. This time, double-click the PASSWORD.XLS workbook file. This opens the workbook and places it on top of the BUDGET.XLS file.
   e. Click the Open button on the Standard toolbar once again, then double-click the PASSWORD2.XLS file (you will need to use the password you assigned in Project 2 to open the file). You now have three Excel workbooks open.

2. **Switch between workbooks**
   a. One way to switch to another open workbook is to use the Windows Taskbar. Click the BUDGET.XLS button on the Taskbar. The BUDGET.XLS workbook now appears.
   b. You can also switch between workbooks using the Windows menu. Click the Windows menu and select PASSWORD.XLS. This brings the PASSWORD.XLS file into view.

Student Workbook
Teach Yourself Excel 2000 VISUALLY

3. **View several files onscreen at the same time**
   a. Open the Windows menu and select Arrange.
   b. Click the Horizontal option, and then click OK.
   c. You now see all three files onscreen. Things look a little crowded, but you can now compare the data in each workbook. You can work on only one workbook at a time. The active workbook's Title bar appears dark blue (unless you have changed your Windows properties). To change active workbooks, click inside another workbook or click another workbook's Title bar.

4. **Close the files**
   a. Close each open workbook file with a click on the workbook's Close button (the button with an X on it at the far-right end of the workbook's Title bar).
   b. To exit Excel completely, click the Close button in the upper-right corner of the Excel program window.

Module 2: Editing Worksheets and Using Formulas

Chapter Coverage

CHAPTER 3	EDIT YOUR WORKSHEETS
CHAPTER 4	WORK WITH FORMULAS AND FUNCTIONS

Tests and Projects Included

Test Title	Chapter Reference
Module 2 Multiple Choice	3 and 4
Module 2 Fill-in-the-Blank	3 and 4
Module 2 Challenge Questions	3 and 4

Project Title	Chapter Reference
Project 1 Applying the AutoSum Function	3 and 4
Project 2 Creating Formulas and Linking Data	3 and 4
Project 3 Using and Displaying Formulas	3 and 4

Materials and Resources

The materials and resources required for successfully completing this module include:

- A computer running Microsoft Excel 2000
- Starter files for the projects
- A color monitor
- A printer, connected to the computer, loaded with paper, online, and ready to print
- At least 30 megabytes of available hard drive space

Student Workbook
Teach Yourself Excel 2000 VISUALLY

Module 2 Objectives

Upon completion of this module, you will be competent in the following areas:

Skill	Chapter
Editing Data	Chapter 3
Deleting Data	Chapter 3
Undoing the Last Change	Chapter 3
Moving Data	Chapter 3
Copying Data	Chapter 3
Linking Data	Chapter 3
Check Spelling	Chapter 3
Using AutoCorrect	Chapter 3
Finding Data	Chapter 3
Finding and Replacing Data	Chapter 3
Inserting Columns and Rows	Chapter 3
Deleting Columns and Rows	Chapter 3
Inserting Cells	Chapter 3
Deleting Cells	Chapter 3
Naming Cells	Chapter 3
Adding a Comment	Chapter 3
Using and Entering Formulas	Chapter 4
Using and Entering Functions	Chapter 4
Using AutoCalculate	Chapter 4
Adding Numbers	Chapter 4
Displaying Formulas	Chapter 4
Copying Formulas	Chapter 4
Locating Errors in Formulas	Chapter 4
Creating Scenarios	Chapter 4

Exercises and Projects

Module 2 Multiple Choice Questions
Please circle the letter in front of the correct response for each question.

1. The term *editing* refers to:
   a. Making changes to data or to the worksheet itself
   b. Opening a file that's been previously saved
   c. Using the Cut button to copy data
   d. All of the above

2. The difference between cutting and copying is:
   a. Cutting and pasting moves data while copying and pasting duplicates data
   b. Cutting adds data while copying duplicates data
   c. Cutting and copying data are basically the same feature
   d. None of the above

3. When making changes to data, which method(s) can be used?
   a. Double-clicking in the cell and making necessary changes
   b. Clicking in the desired cell and then clicking in the Formula bar to make changes
   c. Click in a cell, typing the correct data, and pressing Enter
   d. All of the above

4. How can you remove data from a cell?
   a. Select the cell, press the Delete key
   b. Select the cell and type **Remove**
   c. You can click the Edit menu and then select View to display the data, and then click the Cut button
   d. Both a and b

5. How can data be moved using the mouse?
   a. Hold down the CTRL key as you drag the selected data
   b. Select the cell containing the data you wish to move and click the Copy button
   c. Select the cell containing the data you wish to move, place your mouse pointer over the cell border until it becomes an arrow, and drag the data to a new location
   d. Select the cell containing the data you wish to move, place your mouse pointer over the cell border until it becomes a plus sign, and drag the data to a new location

Student Workbook
Teach Yourself Excel 2000 VISUALLY

6. The Clipboard toolbar appears when you:
   a. Copy or cut more than one piece of data using the Cut or Copy buttons on the Standard toolbar
   b. Open the View menu and select Toolbars, Clipboard
   c. Drag the selected data from one place to another on the worksheet
   d. Both a and b

7. Spell Check will find:
   a. Unrecognized words
   b. Misspelled words
   c. A misused word such as Too versus Two
   d. Both a and b

8. AutoCorrect performs the following function:
   a. This feature corrects frequently misspelled words
   b. This feature displays the correct SUM, AVERAGE, or COUNT of the selected cells
   c. This feature Finds and Replaces existing data
   d. None of the above

9. AutoCalculate performs the following action:
   a. This feature finds frequently misspelled words and corrects them
   b. This feature displays the correct SUM, AVERAGE, or COUNT of the selected cells
   c. This feature Finds and Replaces existing data
   d. None of the above

10. The Find feature performs the following function:
    a. This feature finds frequently misspelled words and corrects them
    b. This feature displays the correct SUM, AVERAGE, or COUNT of the selected cells
    c. Replaces existing data
    d. None of the above

11. To insert a row, you would use which of the following features:
    a. Select the row in which you want the row to be inserted, click the Insert menu, and then select Rows
    b. Click the Insert menu and then select Cells
    c. Click the Insert menu and then select Rows
    d. Select the column in which you want the column to be inserted, click the Insert menu, and then select Columns

12. When inserting cells:
    a. Select the cells where you want the new cells to be inserted, click the Insert menu, and then select Cells
    b. Click the Insert menu and then select Cells
    c. Click the Insert menu and then select Rows
    d. Select the row in which you want the row to be inserted, click the Insert menu, and then select Rows

13. When entering a formula:
    a. You should enter the cell reference instead of the actual data
    b. Enter * when you want to multiply
    c. Enter / when you want to divide
    d. All of the above

14. If a cell contained the formula =30/(10+20)+40, the answer would be:
    a. 41
    b. ⅔
    c. 63
    d. 2.25

15. If a cell contains the function =SUM(A5:A7) and the data in A5 is 3, the data in A6 is 5, and the data in A7 is 42, the answer would be:
    a. 50
    b. 45
    c. 8
    d. None of the above

16. To change a formula, you could:
    a. Double-click in the cell and edit the formula
    b. Select the cell, type the correct formula, and press Enter
    c. Both a and b
    d. None of the above

17. The MIN function would find:
    a. 10 in the list of numbers 25, 45, 67, 78, 91, 10
    b. 25 in the list of numbers 25, 45, 67, 78, 91, 10
    c. 45 in the list of numbers 25, 45, 67, 78, 91, 10
    d. 91 in the list of numbers 25, 45, 67, 78, 91, 10

Student Workbook
Teach Yourself Excel 2000 VISUALLY

18. The MAX function would find:
    a. 10 in the list of numbers 25, 45, 67, 78, 91, 10
    b. 25 in the list of numbers 25, 45, 67, 78, 91, 10
    c. 45 in the list of numbers 25, 45, 67, 78, 91, 10
    d. 91 in the list of numbers 25, 45, 67, 78, 91, 10

19. The Count function would find:
    a. 6 in the list of numbers 25, 45, 67, 78, 91, 10
    b. 25 in the list of numbers 25, 45, 67, 78, 91, 10
    c. 45 in the list of numbers 25, 45, 67, 78, 91, 10
    d. 91 in the list of numbers 25, 45, 67, 78, 91, 10

20. To display formulas within worksheet cells, you can:
    a. Select the Formulas option on the View tab of the Options dialog box
    b. Press CTRL + ~
    c. Both a and b
    d. None of the above

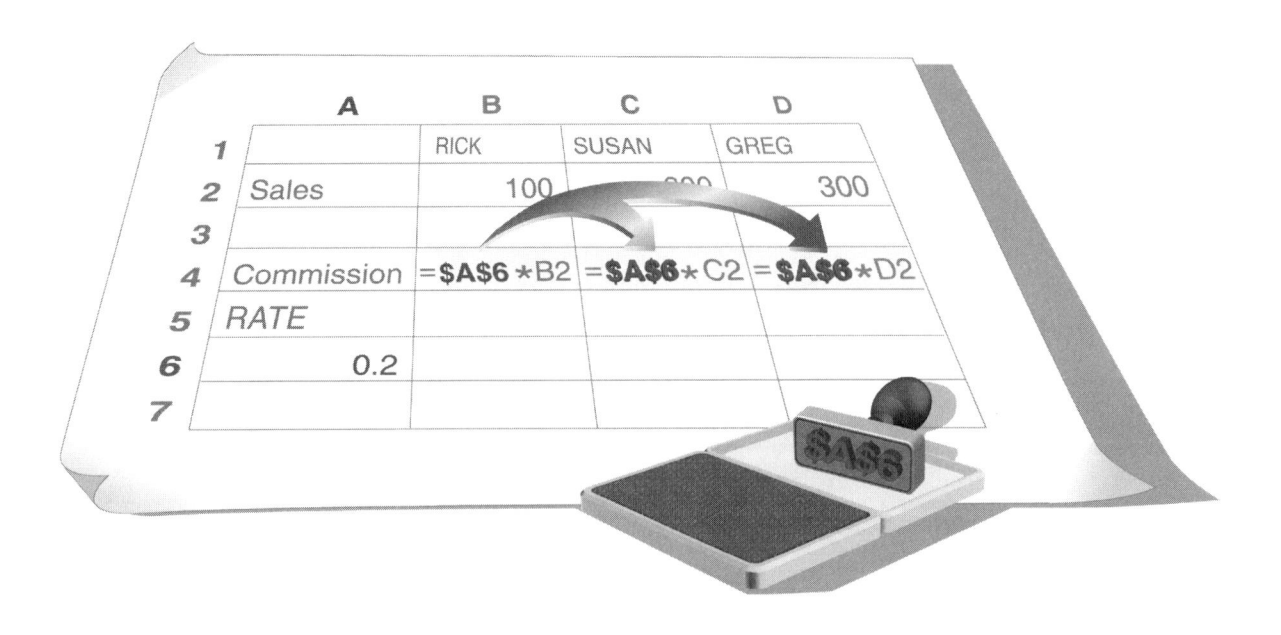

MODULE 2
EXERCISES AND PROJECTS

WORD LIST

#DIV/0
Absolute
AutoCalculate
Clipboard Toolbar
Comment
Copy
CTRL
Cut
Drag
Error
Find
Find Next
Insert
Linked Data
Name Box
Range Name
Relative
Replace
Replace All

Module 2 Fill-in-the-Blank Questions

Select the appropriate word from the list to fill in the blanks:

1. If #NAME? appears in a cell, there is an _____ in the formula.

2. If a formula is divided by a zero (0) value, _____ will appear in a cell.

3. To change a formula when copying it to other cells, you would use _____ referencing.

4. To keep a function absolutely the same when copying it, you would use _____ referencing.

5. Formulas can be displayed in a worksheet by holding down the _____ and pressing the ~ key.

6. _____ will display quick results for six types of functions, including: Sum, Average, Count, Count Nums, Max, and Min. They are displayed on the status bar.

7. A _____ can provide detailed information about cell data.

8. Assigning a _____ to a group of cells makes them easier to remember when creating formulas and functions.

9. Use the _____ to cut or copy two or more data items in a worksheet.

10. To delete several non-consecutive rows at the same time, you would first press and hold down the _____ key and click the numbers of the rows you want to delete and then go up to the Menu and choose Delete.

11. To quickly change the width of a column, _____ the edge of the column heading to the desired width.

Student Workbook
Teach Yourself Excel 2000 VISUALLY

12. To name a group of cells, first select the cells, and then click inside the _____ and enter a range name.

13. The _____ command will put new data into all occurrences of a word or number that Excel was told to find.

14. After Excel has located one cell containing the data you've told it to Find, you would click the _____ button to locate the next cell containing this data.

15. _____ changes when the data in the original cell changes.

	A	B	C	D
1		Jan	Feb	Mar
2	Product 1	2345	4343	4343
3	Product 2	6543	7897	7897
4	Product 3	3423	2848	2848
5		=B2+B3+B4	=C2+C3+C4	=D2+D3+D4

28

Module 2 Challenge Questions

Please use a sentence or a short paragraph to answer the following questions:

1. Describe, in order, the steps necessary to move data from one cell to another.

2. Explain Linking and give an example.

3. Describe the types of words that Excel might find during Spell Check for which you would want to use the Ignore All button.

4. How would you add a frequently misspelled word to AutoCorrect?

5. Explain the Find and Replace feature and how to start this feature.

6. How do you insert a function into your worksheet?

7. Explain the purpose of Comments and give an example of when you would add one.

Student Workbook
Teach Yourself Excel 2000 VISUALLY

8. Explain the differences between absolute and relative reference.

_____
_____

9. How can a comment be deleted from a cell?

_____
_____

10. What has happened if you see #REF! appear in a cell?

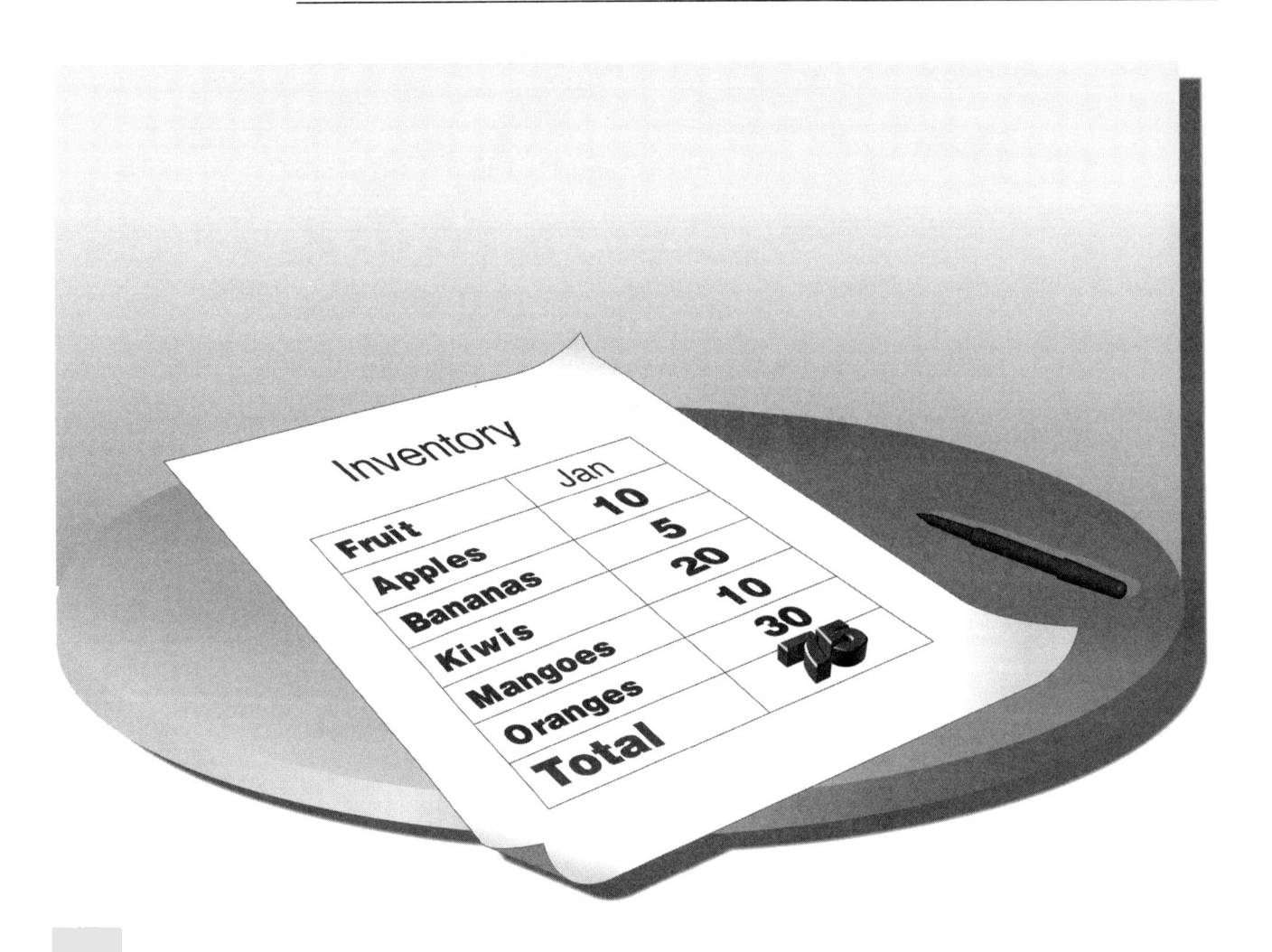

_____
_____

MODULE 2
EXERCISES AND PROJECTS

Project #1: Applying the AutoSum Function

To practice working with functions, reopen the BUDGET.XLS workbook you created in Module 1 and apply the AutoSum function to each row of data. You can do this by applying the function once, and then copying it into the other cells.

Scenario:

As CFO for The Pet Mart, you need to reopen your semiannual budget and total each department's budget information.

Student Name

Teach Yourself Excel 2000 VISUALLY

Module 2 Project 1

The Pet Mart
Semi-Annual Budget

	January	February	March	April	May	June	
Department 1	53.5	57.35	61.2	65.05	68.9	72.75	378.75
Department 2	65	68.25	71.5	74.75	78	81.25	438.75
Department 3	99	107.3	115.6	123.9	132.2	140.5	718.5
Department 4	45.5	42.25	39	35.75	32.5	29.25	224.25
Department 5	45	46.75	48.5	50.25	52	53.75	296.25
Department 6	67	69.25	71.5	73.75	76	78.25	435.75

What you'll need:

A computer running Windows 95 or 98 and Microsoft Excel 2000
A printer, connected to the computer, with paper, online, and ready to print

What to do:

1. **Open the BUDGET.XLS file**
   a. Start Excel and click the Open button on the Standard toolbar.
   b. Locate and double-click the BUDGET2.XLS file you created in Module 1.

2. **Edit the text**
   a. Edit the text in cell A5 to read "Module 2 Project 1."

3. **Apply the AutoSum function**
   a. Click inside cell H11.
   b. Click the AutoSum button on the Standard toolbar and press Enter.
   c. The figures for Department 1 are automatically summed, and the results appear in cell H11.

4. Copy the formula
   a. Select cell H11.
   b. Move your mouse pointer over the cell's fill handle and drag down to cell H16.
   c. The formula is copied to each of the selected cells.

5. Save the workbook
   a. Open the File menu and select Save As.
   b. When the Save As dialog box opens, type **BUDGET2** and then press Enter to save the workbook.

6. Print the workbook
   a. Make sure your printer is turned on, with paper loaded in the appropriate tray.
   b. Click the Print button on the Standard toolbar.

7. Close Excel
   a. Open the File menu and choose Exit.

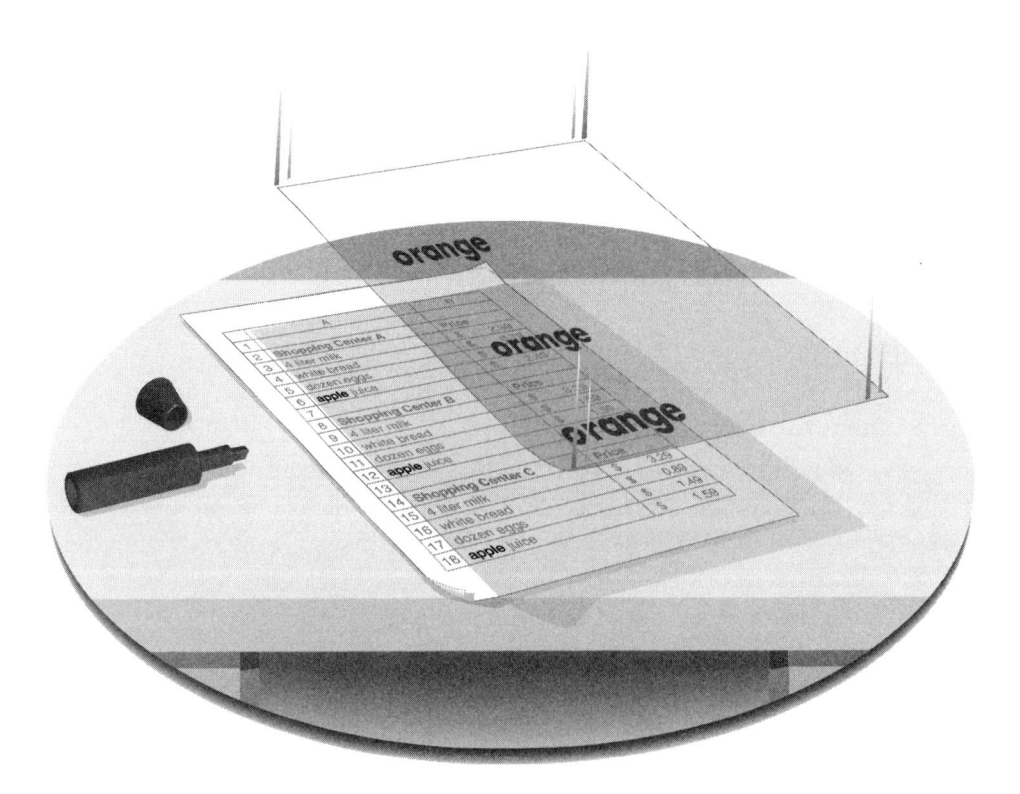

Project #2: Creating Formulas and Linking Data

In this project, you will practice entering formulas and linking data.

Scenario:

Your company, the Sunnyside Restaurant, is a growing pizza business. You want to track the increase in business from last year to this year. Therefore, you will first add functions to total the data and link data in the worksheet.

Student's Name					
Teach Yourself Excel 2000 Visually					
Module 2 Project 2					
	SUNNYSIDE RESTAURANT				
Pizza Sales					
Item	YEAR ENDING 1999	YEAR ENDING 2000	Year Ending 1999:	$ 44,700.00
			Year Ending 2000:	$ 51,200.00
Cheese	$ 15,000.00	$ 16,545.00		
Pepperoni	$ 15,750.00	$ 17,550.00		
Sausage	$ 9,000.00	$ 10,150.00		
Veggie	$ 3,450.00	$ 5,555.00		
Anchovy	$ 1,500.00	$ 1,400.00		
Total	$ 44,700.00	$ 51,200.00		

What you'll need:

A computer running Windows 95 or 98 and Microsoft Excel 2000
A printer, connected to the computer, with paper, online, and ready to print

What to do:

1. **Open the EDIT.XLS workbook**
    a. Start Excel, and then click the Open button.
    b. Double-click the EDIT.XLS workbook file name.

2. **Enter the data**
    a. Type your name in cell A1 and press Enter twice.
    b. Type **Teach Yourself Excel 2000 VISUALLY** in cell A3 and press Enter twice.
    c. Type **Module 2 Project 2** in cell A5 and press Enter twice.

Student Workbook
Teach Yourself Excel 2000 VISUALLY

3. **Enter functions**
   a. Enter a formula in cell B18 that will sum the values in cells B13 through B17. Your formula might look like this: =SUM(B13:B17).
   b. Enter a formula in cell C18 that will sum the values in cells C13 through C17.

4. **Link the data**
   a. Link the following cells:
      G11 to B18
      G12 to C18

5. **Save the workbook**
   a. Open the File menu and choose Save As.
   b. When the Save As dialog box opens, type **EDIT2** and then press Enter to save the workbook.

6. **Print the workbook**
   a. Make sure your printer is turned on, with paper loaded in the appropriate tray.
   b. Click the Print button on the Standard toolbar.

7. **Close Excel**
   a. Open the File menu and click Exit.

MODULE 2
EXERCISES AND PROJECTS

Project #3: Using and Displaying Formulas

In this last project, you'll create formulas for several columns of data, and then show the formulas in the cells.

Scenario:

You've been asked to create a worksheet displaying costs and income for the ALL CITIES CONVENTION for the past two years. You will then make an estimate as to this year's cost and income for the convention. Finally, you will display the formula to double-check for accuracy.

Student's Name				
Teach Yourself Excel 2000 Vis				
Module 2 Project 3				
		ALL CITIES CONVENTION		
Costs				
Item	YEAR ENDING 1998	YEAR ENDING 1999	PROJECT COSTS FOR 2000	
Furniture	1234	2110	2200	
Printing	1388	2259	2400	
Rentals	1542	2408	2600	
Decorations	1696	2557	2800	
Food	1850	2706	3000	
Total	=SUM(B13:B17)	=SUM(C13:C17)	=SUM(D13:D17)	
Income				
Item	YEAR ENDING 1998	YEAR ENDING 1999	PROJECT INCOME FOR 2000	
Furniture	1234	2110	2200	
Printing	1388	2259	2400	
Rentals	1542	2408	2600	
Decorations	1696	2557	2800	
Food	1850	2706	3000	
Total	=SUM(B24:B28)	=SUM(C24:C28)	=SUM(D24:D28)	

What to do:

1. Open the FUNCTION.XLS workbook

   a. Start Excel, and then click the Open button on the Standard toolbar.

   b. Double-click the FUNCTION.XLS workbook to open the file.

Student Workbook
Teach Yourself Excel 2000 VISUALLY

2. **Enter the formulas**
   a. Type your name in cell A1 and press Enter twice on the keyboard.
   b. Type **Teach Yourself Excel 2000 VISUALLY** and press Enter twice on the keyboard.
   c. Type **Module 2 Project 3** and press Enter twice on the keyboard.
   d. Enter formulas into cells B18, B30, C18, C30, D18, and D30 that total the values in the rows above.

3. **Display formulas**
   a. Display the formulas on your screen.

4. **Save the workbook**
   a. Open the File menu and choose Save As.
   b. When the Save As dialog box opens, type **FUNCTION2** and then press Enter to save the workbook.

5. **Print the workbook**
   a. Make sure your printer is turned on, with paper loaded in the appropriate tray.
   b. Click the Print button on the Standard toolbar.

6. **Close Excel**
   a. Open the File menu and choose Exit.

Taking It Even Further

Start the Excel program again, and then reopen the workbook you created in Project 3. Create average formulas for rows 19 and 31. *Hint:* Use the AVERAGE function. For example, the formula for cell B19 would be =AVERAGE(B13:B17).

Module 3: Viewing and Formatting Workbooks

Chapter Coverage

CHAPTER 5 CHANGE YOUR SCREEN DISPLAY
CHAPTER 6 FORMAT YOUR WORKSHEETS

Tests and Projects Included

Test Title	Chapter Reference
Module 3 Multiple Choice	5 and 6
Module 3 Fill-in-the-Blank	5 and 6
Module 3 Challenge Questions	5 and 6

Project Title	Chapter Reference
Project 1 Changing the Screen Display	5 and 6
Project 2 Formatting Data	5 and 6
Project 3 Centering Data Across Columns	5 and 6

Materials and Resources

The materials and resources required for successfully completing this module include:

- A computer running Microsoft Excel 2000
- Starter files for the projects
- A color monitor
- A printer, connected to the computer, loaded with paper, online, and ready to print
- At least 30 megabytes of available hard drive space

Student Workbook
Teach Yourself Excel 2000 VISUALLY

Module 3 Objectives

Upon completion of this module, you will be competent in the following areas:

Skill	Chapter
Zooming In or Out	Chapter 5
Displaying a Full Screen	Chapter 5
Displaying a Toolbar	Chapter 5
Hiding a Toolbar	Chapter 5
Hiding Columns	Chapter 5
Hiding Rows	Chapter 5
Freezing Rows and Columns	Chapter 5
Splitting a Worksheet	Chapter 5
Changing Column Width	Chapter 6
Changing Row Height	Chapter 6
Using Bold, Italic, and Underline	Chapter 6
Changing Horizontal Alignment of Data	Chapter 6
Changing Number Format	Chapter 6
Indenting Data	Chapter 6
Centering Across Columns	Chapter 6
Wrapping Text in Cells	Chapter 6
Changing Vertical Alignment of Data	Chapter 6
Rotating Data in Cells	Chapter 6
Adding Borders	Chapter 6
Changing Colors	Chapter 6
Copying Formats	Chapter 6
Clearing Formats	Chapter 6
Applying Conditional Formats	Chapter 6
Quickly Applying a Design	Chapter 6

Module 3
Exercises and Projects

Exercises and Projects

Module 3 Multiple Choice Questions
Please circle the letter in front of the correct response for each question.

1. Excel offers several ready-to-use designs you can apply to format worksheet cells. What's the name of this feature?
    a. AutoDesign
    b. AutoComplete
    c. AutoFormat
    d. None of the above

2. Conditional Formatting refers to:
    a. Having Excel apply formats to data when the data meets a condition
    b. Applying instant formats to a worksheet using the AutoDesign feature
    c. Having Excel display a message when new formats are applied
    d. All of the above

3. Which sequence of menu commands would you choose if you want to remove all formats within a certain cell and start over?
    a. Edit, Delete
    b. Edit, Clear, All
    c. Edit, Clear, Formats
    d. Edit, Clear, Contents

4. If you want to apply the same format to several locations, how can you keep the Format Painter tool active?
    a. Double-click the Format Painter button
    b. Right-click the Format Painter button
    c. Click once on the Format Painter button
    d. Both a and b

5. To remove the background color of a cell, which of the following should you do?
    a. Change the background color to White
    b. Change the background color to Automatic
    c. Change the background color to No Fill
    d. Change the background color to None

Student Workbook
Teach Yourself Excel 2000 VISUALLY

6. To remove text color, which of the following should you do?
   a. Change the text color to White
   b. Change the text color to No Line
   c. Change the text color to Automatic
   d. Change the text color to None

7. The following borders can be added to a cell:
   a. Single line top border
   b. Double line bottom border
   c. Cell outline
   d. All of the above

8. Excel allows the data to be rotated within a cell at the following angles:
   a. 45 degrees
   b. 90 degrees
   c. –90 degrees
   d. All of the above

9. Changing the way Excel aligns data between the top and bottom edges of a cell is referred to as:
   a. Horizontal alignment
   b. Vertical alignment
   c. Bottom alignment
   d. Top alignment

10. To display multiple lines of text within a cell, you could:
    a. Select the Wrap Text option
    b. Select the Top Alignment option
    c. Select the Bottom Alignment option
    d. None of the above

11. Which of these horizontal alignments can you apply in Excel?
    a. Align data to the left within a cell
    b. Align data to the right within a cell
    c. Center data across columns
    d. All of the above

12. Adding a number format refers to which of the following?
   a. Displaying dollar signs and decimal places to numbers
   b. Changing the background color of a cell containing numbers
   c. Changing the color of numerical data
   d. Both b and c

13. You can enhance the appearance of data by changing which of the following?
   a. Font
   b. Style
   c. Size
   d. All of the above

14. To have Excel fit the longest item in a column, you need to do the following:
   a. Place the mouse pointer over the right edge of the column heading and drag to the right or left
   b. Place the mouse pointer over the left side of the column heading and drag to the right or left
   c. Place the mouse pointer over the right edge of the column heading and double-click
   d. Place the mouse pointer over the left side of the column heading and double-click

15. Which Excel feature can you use to enlarge or descrease the view of the worksheet?
   a. Full Screen view
   b. The Zoom button on the Standard toolbar
   c. The Zoom command on the Edit menu
   d. Both b and c

16. The Freeze feature is designed to:
   a. Freeze columns or rows so that they will not move
   b. Divide the worksheet into two sections, allowing you to scroll in each section
   c. Both a and b
   d. None of the above

17. You may want to hide a column because:
   a. The column contains confidential information
   b. Hiding a column is safer than protecting the workbook
   c. Hidden columns can be redisplayed only with a password
   d. Both b and c

Student Workbook
Teach Yourself Excel 2000 VISUALLY

18. Which two toolbars are automatically displayed when you start the Excel program and share the same row onscreen?
   a. Standard and Formatting toolbars
   b. Standard and Web toolbars
   c. Standard and Chart toolbars
   d. None of the above

19. The steps to unhide a row are as follows:
   a. Click Format, Column, Unhide
   b. Place your mouse pointer over the bottom side of the row heading and double-click
   c. Select the rows above and below hidden row, and then click Format, row, unhide.
   d. Place your mouse pointer over the top side of the row heading and double-click

20. The following feature(s) can be found in the Format Cells dialog box:
   a. Text Color
   b. Alignment
   c. Borders
   d. All of the above

Module 3
Exercises and Projects

WORD LIST

Alignment
AutoFormat
Background
Bold, Italic, and Underline
Conditional Formatting
Enter Data Across Columns
Fit Longest Item
Fit Tallest Item
Font
Format Painter
Formats
Freeze
Gridlines
Hiding
Horizontal
Indent
Rotate
Shrink to Fit
Split
Vertical
Wrap Text
Zoom

Module 3 Fill-in-the-Blank Questions

Select the appropriate word from the list to fill in the blanks:

1. _____ are predefined number and text formats, backgrounds and borders, and other formatting styles you can apply to create a professional-looking worksheet.

2. To have the background color of a cell display in Blue when a certain condition is met, you could use _____.

3. _____, such as background color, can be removed from a cell without removing the data.

4. Formats can by copied using the _____ button on the Standard toolbar.

5. Use the _____ feature to magnify your view of worksheet cells.

6. _____ can be used to print the worksheet data with lines instead of using borders.

7. If you wanted to use a 45-degree alignment for selected cells, you would _____ the data in cells.

8. Centering data within a cell between the top and bottom edges is referred to as _____ alignment.

9. Excel can wrap text within a cell or it can _____, which reduces the font size until the text fits.

10. You can _____ to center titles over the data.

11. _____ data within a cell allows you to offset the data from the cell's edge.

12. Superscript, subscript, and strikethrough can be found on the _____ tab of the Format Cells dialog box.

13. Changing the Left, Center, or Right position of data between the left and right cell border is referred to as _____ alignment.

14. Three common features you can add to text and numbers to emphasize worksheet data are _____.

43

Student Workbook
Teach Yourself Excel 2000 VISUALLY

15. Double-clicking the right edge of a column heading to change the column width is referred to as _____.

16. Double-clicking the bottom edge of a row heading to change the row height is referred to as _____.

17. To view two parts of a worksheet at one time and scroll in each section, you would _____ the worksheet.

18. To view two parts of a worksheet at one time and allow scrolling only in the right section, you would use the _____ feature.

19. To prevent viewing of confidential data contained in a column, you can _____ the column.

20. _____ a toolbar allows more of the worksheet data to be viewed onscreen.

Module 3 Challenge Questions

Please use a sentence or a short paragraph to answer the following questions:

1. Describe, in order, the steps necessary to apply one of Excel's AutoFormats.

2. Explain Conditional Formatting and give an example.

3. When would you use Clear Formats instead of Clear Contents?

4. What is the difference between vertical and horizontal alignment?

5. Explain the differences between Wrap Text and Shrink to Fit.

6. How could you center titles over your data?

7. Give three examples of Number formats.

Student Workbook
Teach Yourself Excel 2000 VISUALLY

8. List the steps for freezing a worksheet.

_____

_____

9. Describe three methods for viewing a larger portion of your worksheet without changing the worksheet itself.

_____

_____

10. How do you view additional buttons on the Standard or Formatting toolbars?

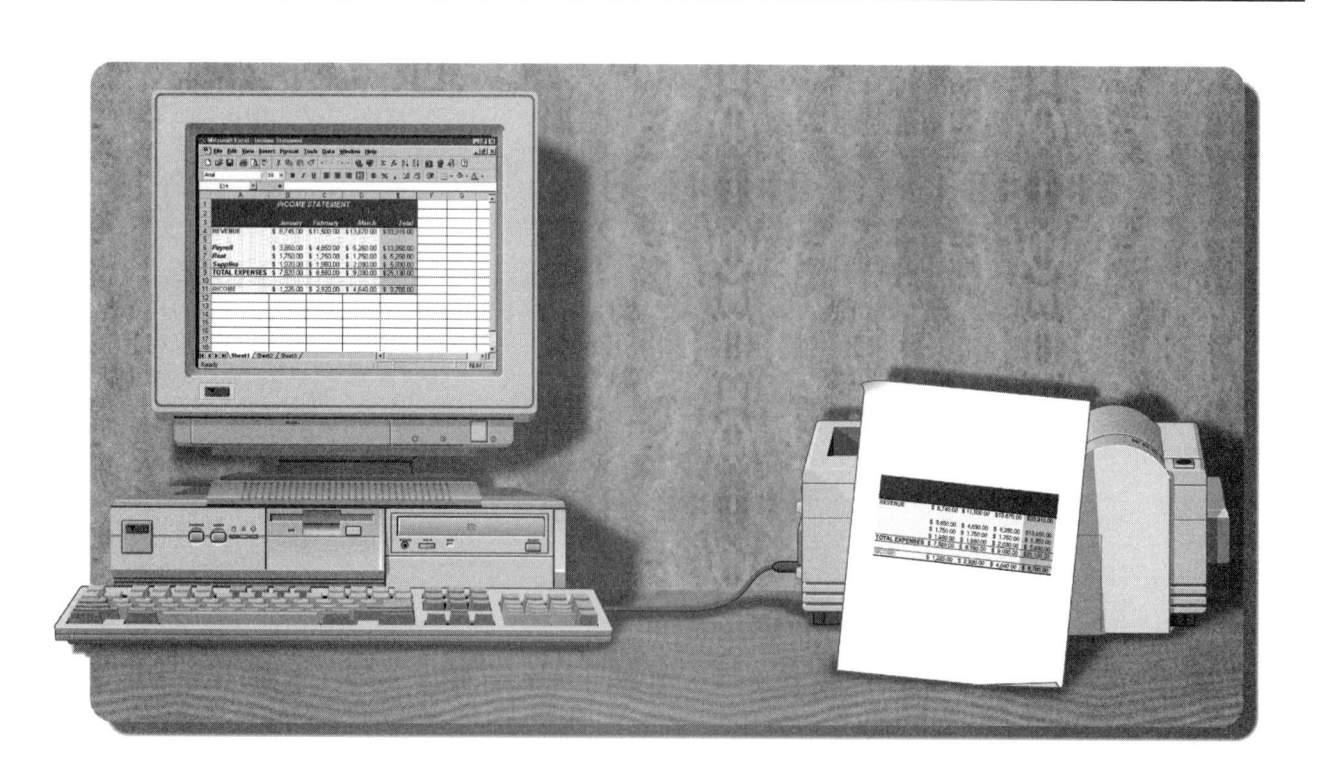

_____

_____

Module 3
Exercises and Projects

Project #1: Changing the Screen Display
In this project, you will practice hiding and freezing columns.

Scenario:
You are the Chief Financial Officer for Trendy Resorts. The time has come to print out the year-end information for the company's lenders. As the banks are requesting only sales information at this point, you need to hide the columns containing Net Income. You then decide to make the worksheet easier to read by freezing column A.

What you'll need:
A computer running Windows 95 or 98 and Microsoft Excel 2000
A printer, connected to the computer, with paper, online, and ready to print

What to do:

1. **Open the VIEW.XLS file**
   a. Start Excel and click the Open button on the Standard toolbar.
   b. Double-click the VIEW.XLS file name.

2. **Enter data**
   a. Type your name in cell A1 and press Enter twice on the keyboard.
   b. Type **Teach Yourself Excel 2000 VISUALLY** and press Enter twice.
   c. Type **Module 3 Project 1** in cell A5.

3. **Hide columns**
   a. Hide columns O and P.

4. **Freeze a column**
   a. Freeze column A.

Student Workbook
Teach Yourself Excel 2000 VISUALLY

5. Save the workbook
   a. Open the File menu and select Save As.
   b. When the Save As dialog box opens, type **VIEW2** and then press Enter to save the workbook.

6. Print the workbook
   a. Make sure your printer is turned on, with paper loaded in the appropriate tray.
   b. Click the Print button on the Standard toolbar.

7. Close Excel
   a. Open the File menu and click Exit.

Student's Name

Teach Yourself Excel 2000 Visually

Module 3 Project 1

Trendy Resort Project Sales
First Year

	Jan	Feb	Mar	Apr	May
Division 1	$ 56,880.00	$ 57,332.00	$ 57,784.00	$ 58,236.00	$ 58,688.00
Division 2	62,445.00	61,333.00	60,221.00	59,109.00	57,997.00
Division 3	$ 56,880.00	$ 57,332.00	$ 57,784.00	$ 58,236.00	$ 58,688.00
Division 4	62,445.00	61,333.00	60,221.00	59,109.00	57,997.00
Division 5	$ 56,880.00	$ 57,332.00	$ 57,784.00	$ 58,236.00	$ 58,688.00
Division 6	62,445.00	61,333.00	60,221.00	59,109.00	57,997.00
Division 7	$ 56,880.00	$ 57,332.00	$ 57,784.00	$ 58,236.00	$ 58,688.00
	$ 414,855.00	$ 413,327.00	$ 411,799.00	$ 410,271.00	$ 408,743.00

Project #2: Formatting Data

Use this project to practice formatting cells in a worksheet, including changing style, size, background color, and cell borders.

Scenario:

Your company, International Imports, is giving a presentation of its Year 2001 Financial Statements. A professional-looking worksheet is extremely important as it will be distributed to the shareholders. You decide to format the worksheet as shown in the following illustration.

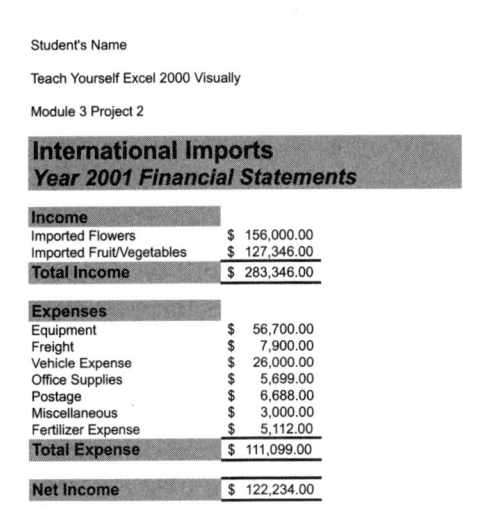

Student's Name

Teach Yourself Excel 2000 Visually

Module 3 Project 2

International Imports
Year 2001 Financial Statements

Income	
Imported Flowers	$ 156,000.00
Imported Fruit/Vegetables	$ 127,346.00
Total Income	$ 283,346.00

Expenses	
Equipment	$ 56,700.00
Freight	$ 7,900.00
Vehicle Expense	$ 26,000.00
Office Supplies	$ 5,699.00
Postage	$ 6,688.00
Miscellaneous	$ 3,000.00
Fertilizer Expense	$ 5,112.00
Total Expense	$ 111,099.00

Net Income	$ 122,234.00

What to do:

1. **Open the FORMAT.XLS file**
    a. Start Excel and click the Open button on the Standard toolbar.
    b. Double-click the FORMAT.XLS file.

2. **Enter and format data**
    a. Click inside cell A1 and type your name and press Enter twice.
    b. Type **Teach Yourself Excel 2000 VISUALLY** and press Enter twice.
    c. Type **Module 3 Project 2** and press Enter once.
    d. Format the worksheet as shown in the illustration at the beginning of this project and as described in the following table.

Cell(s)	Format	Cell Background	Size
A7:D7	Bold text	Gray	18
A8:D8	Bold italic text	Gray	16
A10	Bold text	Gray	12
A13	Bold text	Gray	12
A15	Bold text	Gray	12
A23	Bold text	Gray	12
A25	Bold text	Gray	12
B13	Top and bottom single border		
B23	Top and bottom single border		
B25	Top single border and double underline bottom border		
B11:B25	Currency Style number format		

3. **Save the workbook**
   a. Open the File menu and select Save As.
   b. When the Save As dialog box opens, type **FORMAT2** and then press Enter to save the workbook.

4. **Print the workbook**
   a. Make sure your printer is turned on, with paper loaded in the appropriate tray.
   b. Click the Print button on the Standard toolbar.

5. **Close Excel**
   a. Open the File menu and select Exit.

Taking It Even Further

Start the Excel program again, and then open the FORMAT2.XLS workbook. Clear all existing formats. Open the AutoFormats dialog box and select a three-dimensional effect for this worksheet.

When you are finished with this project, be sure to save your work, and then exit Excel to prepare the computer for the next user and to free up resources in the computer.

Project #3: Centering Data Across Columns

Use this project to practice centering title data across cells and copying formatting with the Format Painter tool.

Scenario:

As the person in charge of The Pet Mart's budget distribution, you need to polish up the worksheet before handing it out to the other board members. Use Excel's formatting tools to make the presentation easier to read and more presentable.

What you'll need:

A computer running Windows 95 or 98 and Microsoft Excel 2000
A printer, connected to the computer, with paper, online, and ready to print

What to do:

1. **Open the BUDGET.XLS file**
    a. Start Excel and display the Open dialog box.
    b. Double-click the BUDGET.XLS workbook you created back in Project 1 of Module 1.

2. **Edit text**
    a. Type **Module 3 Project 3** in cell A5.

3. **Center data across columns**
    a. Select the title text found in cell A8 and expand the selected range to G8.
    b. Center data across columns with the Merge and Center command.
    c. With the cells still selected, format the text to bold, underlined, 16-point size.

4. **Apply number formatting**
    a. Select the budget data in cells B11:G16.
    b. Change the number formatting to Currency Style.

Student Workbook
Teach Yourself Excel 2000 VISUALLY

5. **Apply text formatting**
   a. Select row 10 on the worksheet.
   b. Center the text, make it bold, and change the color to red.
   c. Select cell A7 and make the text bold, 20-point size.

6. **Copy formatting**
   a. Select cell A11.
   b. Make the text bold, italic, and change the color to blue.
   c. Use the Format Painter button to copy the formatting to cells A12:A16.

7. **Save the workbook**
   a. Open the File menu and choose Save As.
   b. When the Save As dialog box opens, type **BUDGET3** and then press Enter to save the workbook.

8. **Print the workbook**
   a. Make sure your printer is turned on, with paper loaded in the appropriate tray.
   b. Click the Print button on the Standard toolbar.

9. **Close Excel**
   a. Open the File menu and choose Exit.

Student Name

Teach Yourself Excel 2000 VISUALLY

Module 3 Project 3

The Pet Mart
Semi-Annual Budget

	January	February	March	April	May	June
Department 1	$ 53.50	$ 57.35	$ 61.20	$ 65.05	$ 68.90	$ 72.75
Department 2	$ 65.00	$ 68.25	$ 71.50	$ 74.75	$ 78.00	$ 81.25
Department 3	$ 99.00	$ 107.30	$ 115.60	$ 123.90	$ 132.20	$ 140.50
Department 4	$ 45.50	$ 42.25	$ 39.00	$ 35.75	$ 32.50	$ 29.25
Department 5	$ 45.00	$ 46.75	$ 48.50	$ 50.25	$ 52.00	$ 53.75
Department 6	$ 67.00	$ 69.25	$ 71.50	$ 73.75	$ 76.00	$ 78.25

Module 4: Printing and Using Multiple Worksheets

Chapter Coverage

CHAPTER 7 PRINT YOUR WORKSHEETS
CHAPTER 8 WORK WITH MULTIPLE WORKSHEETS

Tests and Projects Included

Test Title	Chapter Reference
Module 4 Multiple Choice	7 and 8
Module 4 Fill-in-the-Blank	7 and 8
Module 4 Challenge Questions	7 and 8

Project Title	Chapter Reference
Project 1 Changing Print Options	7 and 8
Project 2 Using Formulas Across Worksheets	7 and 8

Materials and Resources

The materials and resources required for successfully completing this module include:

- A computer running Microsoft Excel 2000
- Starter files for the projects
- A color monitor
- A printer, connected to the computer, loaded with paper, online, and ready to print
- At least 30 megabytes of available hard drive space

Student Workbook
Teach Yourself Excel 2000 VISUALLY

Module 4 Objectives

Upon completion of this module, you will be competent in the following areas:

Skill	Chapter
Previewing a Worksheet	Chapter 7
Printing a Worksheet	Chapter 7
Setting a Print Area	Chapter 7
Changing Margins	Chapter 7
Centering Data on a Page	Chapter 7
Changing Page Orientation	Chapter 7
Change Print Options	Chapter 7
Inserting a Page Break	Chapter 7
Adding a Header and Footer	Chapter 7
Changing the Size of Printed Data	Chapter 7
Repeating Titles on Printed Pages	Chapter 7
Switching Between Worksheeets	Chapter 8
Inserting a Worksheet	Chapter 8
Deleting a Worksheet	Chapter 8
Renaming a Worksheet	Chapter 8
Moving a Worksheet	Chapter 8
Moving and Copying Data Between Worksheets	Chapter 8
Entering a Formula Across Worksheets	Chapter 8

Exercises and Projects

Module 4 Multiple Choice Questions
Please circle the letter in front of the correct response for each question.

1. To view a worksheet before it's printed, you would select the following option:
   a. Print Screen
   b. Print Preview
   c. Print Setup
   d. None of the above

2. When working with multiple worksheets, you can:
   a. Move data between worksheets
   b. Copy data between worksheets
   c. Enter formulas across worksheets
   d. All of the above

3. If you wanted to give a worksheet a descriptive name to help you locate its information within a workbook, you would:
   a. Move the worksheet to the beginning of the workbook
   b. Copy the worksheet data to the first worksheet
   c. Rename the worksheet
   d. Insert a new worksheet

4. Deleting a worksheet:
   a. Permanently deletes the worksheet from the workbook
   b. Deletes only the data within the worksheet
   c. Is temporary as long as you immediately click the Undo button
   d. Both a and b

5. To insert a worksheet, you simply need to:
   a. Right-click a worksheet tab and choose New
   b. Open the Insert menu and choose Worksheet
   c. Click the New button on the Standard toolbar
   d. All of the above

Student Workbook
Teach Yourself Excel 2000 VISUALLY

6. To repeat titles on printed pages, you first need to:
   a. Select the Sheet tab in the Page Setup dialog box
   b. Select the Sheet tab in the Margins dialog box
   c. Select the Page tab in the Page Setup dialog box
   d. Select the Sheet tab in the Print dialog box

7. The printout of your worksheet shows two rows of data on a second page that you would prefer to be on the first page. What can you do to prevent this from happening?
   a. Change Zoom to a lower setting
   b. Delete the two rows of data
   c. Open the Page Setup dialog box, display the Page tab, select the Fit To option and enter 1 in the Pages Wide By box
   d. Both a and b

8. A header will print:
   a. At the bottom of every other page
   b. Across the bottom of each worksheet in a workbook
   c. Across the top of each page
   d. On the first page only

9. Which Excel feature lets you view how your page breaks fall?
   a. Print Preview
   b. Page Break Preview
   c. Page Layout View
   d. Normal Print View

10. How do you set up Excel to print Comments on the same sheet as the worksheet data?
    a. Open the Margins dialog box and select Comments
    b. Open the Page Setup dialog box, display the Sheet tab, and use the Comments drop-down list to specify an option
    c. Switch to Print Preview and click the Comments button
    d. None of the above

MODULE 4
EXERCISES AND PROJECTS

11. When manually changing the size of printed data, which of the following statements is true?
    a. A percentage over 100 increases the size of printed data
    b. A percentage below 100 decreases the size of printed data
    c. The Adjust To option will need to be selected
    d. All of the above

12. A footer will print:
    a. On the edge of every other page
    b. Across the bottom of each page
    c. Across the top of each worksheet in a workbook
    d. On the first page only

13. How is Landscape orientation printed on a page?
    a. It prints across the widest portion of the page
    b. It prints across the shortest portion of the page
    c. It prints on both sides of the page
    d. Excel can't print Landscape orientation

14. In Excel, you can print:
    a. The active worksheet
    b. A specified print area
    c. The entire workbook
    d. All of the above

15. To quickly print the current worksheet:
    a. Click the Print button on the Standard toolbar
    b. Click the Print Preview button
    c. Click Print from the Sheet tab
    d. None of the above

16. Which of the following is not a print option?
    a. Gridlines
    b. Draft Quality
    c. Comments
    d. Insert Worksheet

17. When you copy a formula from one worksheet to another:
   a. Excel will automatically change the cell reference in the formula for the new location
   b. Excel will change the cell reference in the formula for the new location if they are in absolute value format
   c. The cells are automatically linked
   d. All of the above

18. If ##### appears in a cell:
   a. You will need to increase the column width
   b. The cell formula is incorrect
   c. There is a page break in this cell
   d. None of the above

19. To insert a page break into a worksheet:
   a. Open the View menu and choose Insert
   b. Open the Insert menu and choose Page Break
   c. Press Ctrl + Enter on the keyboard
   d. Right-click and select Break

20. To rename a worksheet tab:
   a. Double-click the tab, type the new name, and press Enter
   b. Select Insert, Name, and enter a name for the worksheet
   c. Choose Format, Worksheet, and enter a name for the worksheet
   d. Select the Worksheet Name box in the Page Setup dialog box

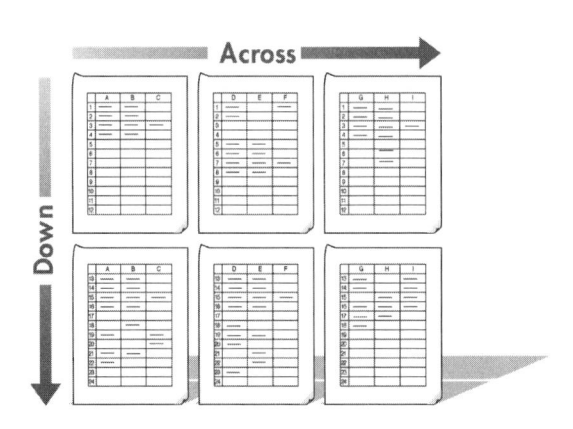

MODULE 4
EXERCISES AND PROJECTS

Module 4 Fill-in-the-Blank Questions
Select the appropriate word from the list to fill in the blanks:

WORD LIST

Automatically
Cell References
Footer
Header
Insert
Landscape
Margin
Moving
Page Break Preview
Page Setup
Permanently
Portrait
Print Area
Print Preview
Rename
Tab

1. If you change a number used in a formula, Excel will _____ recalculate the total.

2. When a formula is copied from one worksheet to another, the _____ will change to reflect the new location if they are not in an absolute reference format.

3. You can reorganize data by _____ a worksheet to a new location within the workbook.

4. To give a worksheet a more descriptive name, you could _____ the worksheet.

5. By default, three worksheets appear in a new workbook. If you need additional worksheets, you could _____ a new worksheet.

6. When a worksheet is deleted, it is removed from the workbook _____.

7. To change print options, open the _____ dialog box.

8. To display the contents of any worksheet, click the worksheet's _____.

9. You would use the _____ feature to view repeated titles before printing.

10. You can display information, such as the workbook title and page number, at the top of each page or your worksheet by using a _____.

11. Each page break in a worksheet can be viewed in the _____ screen.

12. A _____ is the amount of space between data and the edge of the paper.

Student Workbook
Teach Yourself Excel 2000 VISUALLY

13. If you always print the same area of a worksheet, you can set a _____ to print the data quickly.

14. To print on paper taller than it is wide, you would select the _____ option.

15. To print on paper wider than it is tall, you would select the _____ option.

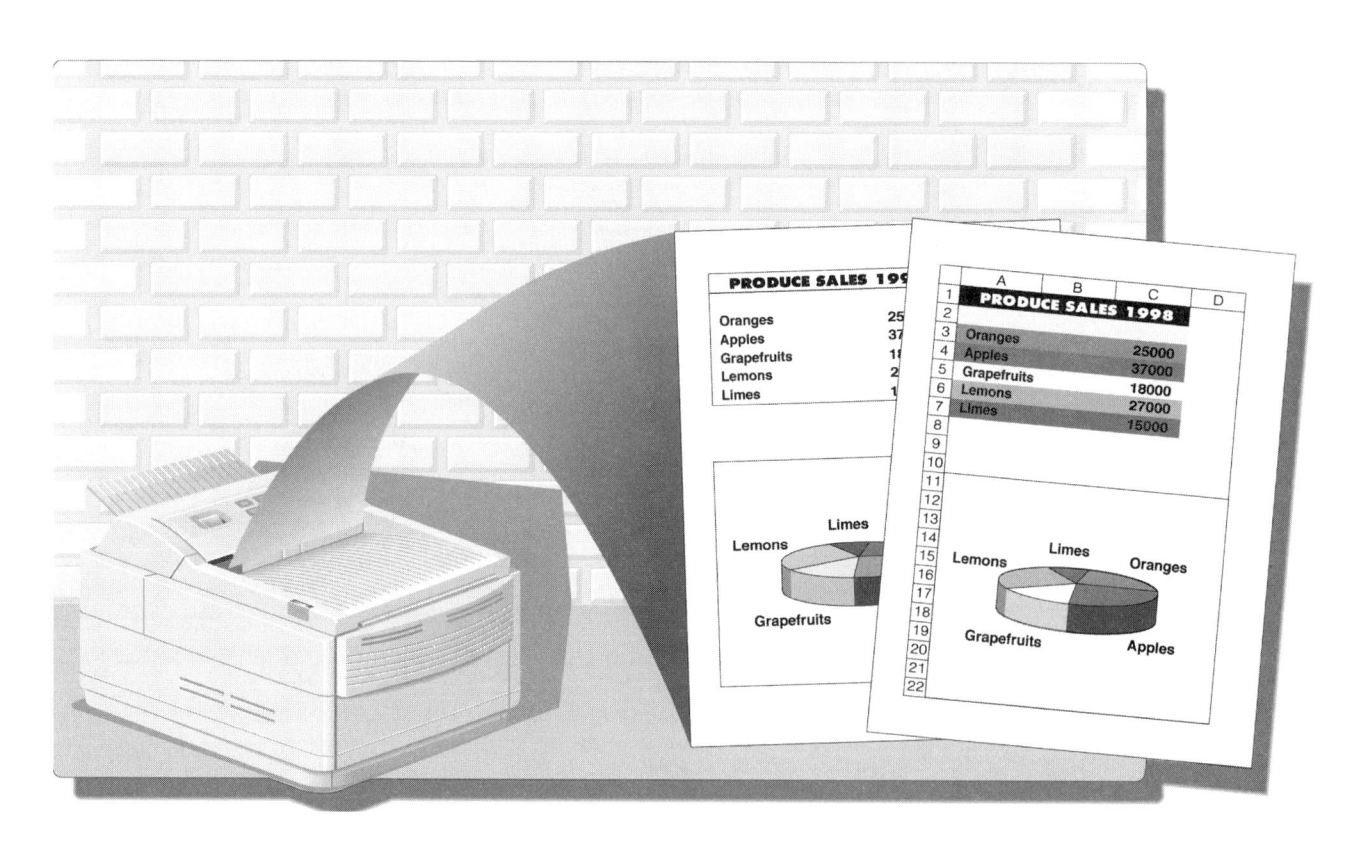

Module 4 Challenge Questions

Please use a sentence or a short paragraph to answer the following questions:

1. Describe, in order, the steps necessary to change Page Orientation.

2. List the steps for printing a Selection of highlighted cells in a worksheet.

3. When would you use Page Break Preview instead of Print Preview?

4. What is the difference between vertical and horizontal page alignment?

5. Why would you enter a formula across worksheets? Give an example.

6. List some reasons why you should always preview a worksheet before printing.

7. You've created a worksheet with vivid colors. However, when you go into Print Preview, it appears in black and white. Why?

Student Workbook
Teach Yourself Excel 2000 VISUALLY

8. If a print area is set for the worksheet and you decide you want to print other data in the worksheet, what can you do?

_____

_____

9. Give two examples of when you might want to change margin settings.

_____

_____

10. Define page break.

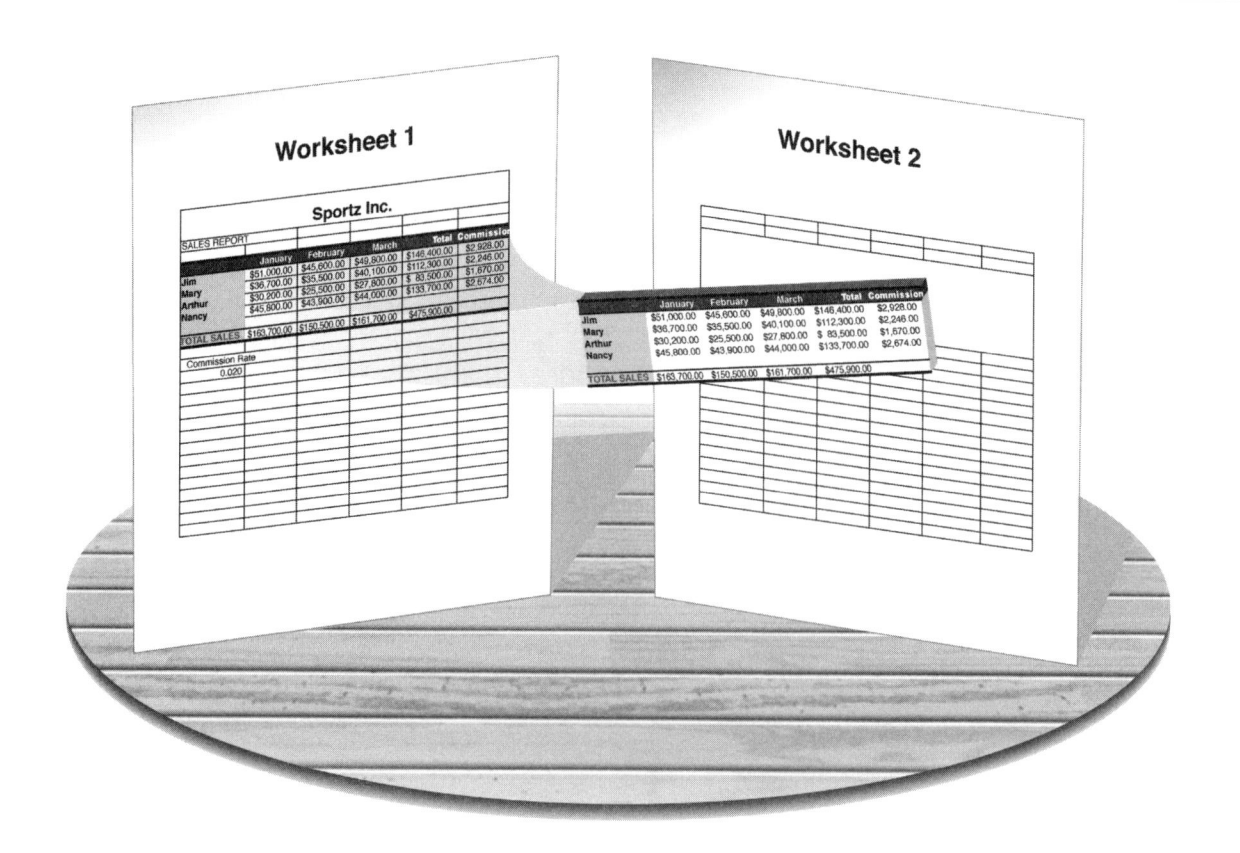

_____

_____

MODULE 4
EXERCISES AND PROJECTS

Project #1: Changing Print Options

In this project, you will practice using several of Excel's print options, including fitting worksheet data to one page and selecting a page orientation. You will also view the worksheet in the Print Preview window.

Scenario:

As the CEO for National Enterprise Project Sales, you need to print the annual report. You want the printout to fit on one page and to appear in Landscape orientation.

Student's Name

Teach Yourself Excel 2000 Visually

Module 4 Project 1

National Enterprise Project Sales

	Jan	Feb	Mar	Apr	May	Jun
Division 1	$ 56,880.00	$ 57,332.00	$ 57,784.00	$ 58,236.00	$ 58,688.00	$ 59,140.00
Division 2	62,445.00	61,333.00	60,221.00	59,109.00	57,997.00	56,885.00
Division 3	$ 56,880.00	$ 57,332.00	$ 57,784.00	$ 58,236.00	$ 58,688.00	$ 59,140.00
Division 4	62,445.00	61,333.00	60,221.00	59,109.00	57,997.00	56,885.00
Division 5	$ 56,880.00	$ 57,332.00	$ 57,784.00	$ 58,236.00	$ 58,688.00	$ 59,140.00
Division 6	62,445.00	61,333.00	60,221.00	59,109.00	57,997.00	56,885.00
Division 7	$ 56,880.00	$ 57,332.00	$ 57,784.00	$ 58,236.00	$ 58,688.00	$ 59,140.00
	$ 414,855.00	$ 413,327.00	$ 411,799.00	$ 410,271.00	$ 408,743.00	$ 407,215.00

What you'll need:

A computer running Windows 95 or 98 and Microsoft Excel 2000
A printer, connected to the computer, with paper, online, and ready to print

What to do:

1. **Open the PRINTING.XLS file**
   a. Start Excel, then click the Open button on the Standard toolbar.
   b. Open the PRINTING.XLS workbook file.

2. **Enter data**
   a. Type your name in cell A1 and press Enter twice on the keyboard.
   b. Type **Teach Yourself Excel 2000 VISUALLY** and press Enter twice.
   c. Type **Module 4 Project 1** in cell A5.

3. **Preview the workbook**
   a. Click the Print Preview button on the Standard toolbar.
   b. View both pages of the worksheet. Use the Zoom tool to magnify your view.
   c. Click the Close button to exit the Print Preview window.

Student Workbook
Teach Yourself Excel 2000 VISUALLY

4. Change Print Options
   a. Open the File menu and select Print.
   b. Use the Page Setup dialog box to change the page orientation to Landscape.
   c. Change the printing to fit on one page.

5. Save the workbook
   a. Open the File menu and select Save As.
   b. When the Save As dialog box opens, type **PRINTING2**, and then press Enter to save the workbook.

6. Preview the workbook again
   a. Click the Print Preview button on the Standard toolbar.
   b. Notice the page displays in Landscape orientation and fits on one page now.
   c. Click Close to exit Print Preview.

7. Print the workbook
   a. Make sure your printer is turned on, with paper loaded in the appropriate tray.
   b. Open the File menu and select Print.
   c. When the Print dialog box opens, click the OK button to print the workbook.

8. Exit Excel
   a. Open the File menu and select Exit.

Project #2: Using Formulas Across Worksheets

Practice using formulas across worksheets in this project.

Scenario:

As the parent of a college student, you are trying to plan the amount of expenses that will be required over a four-year period. Each year's expenses are tracked on a separate worksheet. Use a Summary worksheet to total expenses for seven categories, entering a formula that sums data across worksheets.

What to do:

1. **Open the ORGANIZE.XLS workbook**
   a. Click the Start button on the Taskbar, move the mouse pointer to Programs, and then click Microsoft Excel.
   b. Open the ORGANIZE.XLS workbook file.

2. **Enter data**
   a. Select cell A15 on the First Year tab, type your name, and press Enter twice on the keyboard.
   b. Type **Teach Yourself Excel 2000 VISUALLY** and press Enter twice.
   c. Type **Module 4 Project 2** in cell A19.

3. **Create formulas across worksheets**
   a. Click the Summary worksheet tab.
   b. Use cells B6 through B11 to enter formulas across worksheets that total the expenses in each category for each year's worksheet. (*Hint*: Cell B5 has a formula that adds the totals across worksheets for the Dorm Fee category. Examine it as an example.) Don't forget to begin each formula with an equal sign (=).
   c. Enter a total for the all the expenses in cell B12. (*Hint*: Select cell B12 and click the AutoSum button. Then press Enter.)

4. **Save the workbook**
   a. Open the File menu and select Save As.
   b. When the Save As dialog box opens, type **ORGANIZE2**, and then press Enter to save the workbook.

Student Workbook
Teach Yourself Excel 2000 VISUALLY

5. Print the workbook

  a. Make sure your printer is turned on, with paper loaded in the appropriate tray.

  b. Click the Print button on the Standard toolbar.

6. Exit Excel

  a. Click the Close button on the Excel program window to close the workbook and exit Excel.

Taking It Even Further

Start the Excel program again, and then open the ORGANIZE2.XLS workbook. Apply Currency formats to the data on the Summary worksheet and add a label in cell A12 that reads "Total Expense." In the First Year through Fourth Year worksheets, change Currency formats to appear only on the first row of data and on the totals.

When you are finished with this project, be sure to save your work, and then exit Excel to prepare the computer for the next user and to free up resources in the computer.

College Budget
Summary

Dorm Fee	$ 10,000.00
Tuition	$ 17,600.00
Books	$ 3,025.00
Meals	$ 6,600.00
Clothes	$ 2,400.00
Gas	$ 1,200.00
Misc.	$ 3,000.00
	$ 43,825.00

Module 5: Working with Charts and Graphics

Chapter Coverage

CHAPTER 9 WORK WITH CHARTS
CHAPTER 10 WORK WITH GRAPHICS

Tests and Projects Included

Test Title	Chapter Reference
Module 5 Multiple Choice	9 and 10
Module 5 Fill-in-the-Blank	9 and 10
Module 5 Challenge Questions	9 and 10

Project Title	Chapter Reference
Project 1 Create a Chart	9 and 10
Project 2 Adding Graphics	9 and 10

Materials and Resources

The materials and resources required for successfully completing this module include:

- A computer running Microsoft Excel 2000
- Starter files for the projects
- A color monitor
- A printer, connected to the computer, loaded with paper, online, and ready to print
- At least 30 megabytes of available hard drive space

Student Workbook
Teach Yourself Excel 2000 VISUALLY

Module 5 Objectives

Upon completion of this module, you will be competent in the following areas:

Skill	Chapter
Creating Charts	Chapter 9
Changing Chart Type	Chapter 9
Moving and Sizing a Chart	Chapter 9
Printing a Chart	Chapter 9
Adding Data to a Chart	Chapter 9
Changing the Appearance of Data Series	Chapter 9
Changing Chart Titles	Chapter 9
Rotating Chart Text	Chapter 9
Formatting Chart Text	Chapter 9
Changing the Way Data is Plotted	Chapter 9
Adding a Data Table to a Chart	Chapter 9
Changing View of a 3-D Chart	Chapter 9
Displaying Data in a Map	Chapter 9
Adding an AutoShape	Chapter 10
Adding a Text Box	Chapter 10
Adding Clip Art	Chapter 10
Adding a Picture	Chapter 10
Moving and Sizing a Graphic	Chapter 10
Deleting a Graphic	Chapter 10
Making a Graphic 3-D	Chapter 10
Changing Graphic Color	Chapter 10
Changing Line Color	Chapter 10

Exercises and Projects

Module 5 Multiple Choice Questions
Please circle the letter in front of the correct response for each question.

1. When working with graphics, which of the following feature(s) can be changed?
    a. Line color
    b. Graphic color
    c. Size
    d. All of the above

2. Which part of a chart identifies the color, pattern, or symbol that represents each data series in your chart?
    a. The legend
    b. The X-axis
    c. The Y-axis
    d. The Data series

3. A group of related data representing a row or column of data from your worksheet is referred to as:
    a. The legend
    b. The X-axis
    c. The Y-axis
    d. The Data series

4. Which part of the chart indicates the unit of measure used in your chart?
    a. The legend
    b. The X-axis
    c. The Y-axis
    d. The Data series

5. The feature that takes you step-by-step through the process of creating a chart is the:
    a. Function Wizard
    b. Graphics Wizard
    c. Chart Wizard
    d. Worksheet Wizard

Student Workbook
Teach Yourself Excel 2000 VISUALLY

6. Each time your worksheet data changes:
   a. You will need to create a new chart
   b. You will need to click the Update tool to display the change
   c. The existing chart will update automatically
   d. The existing chart will update after saving the workbook

7. A new chart can be created:
   a. In a new worksheet
   b. As an object in the same worksheet as the data
   c. Both a and b
   d. None of the above

8. If you wanted to select a type of chart that would show percentages, the ideal chart type would be:
   a. A column chart
   b. A line chart
   c. A pie chart
   d. An area chart

9. To see what a chart will look like when it's printed, select:
   a. Print Preview
   b. Chart Preview
   c. Workbook Preview
   d. Normal Print View

10. To select a chart:
    a. Click a blank area in the chart
    b. Press Ctrl + S
    c. Press Ctrl + P
    d. Click a cell outside the chart

11. After a chart is created, you can:
    a. Add new data to the chart
    b. Change the chart type
    c. Add titles
    d. All of the above

12. You can change the color of:
    a. The chart background
    b. Data series
    c. Background of the chart legend
    d. All of the above

13. As you type a new title for a chart, it is displayed in the:
    a. Formula bar
    b. Title box
    c. Print Preview screen
    d. Title bar

14. Excel provides many ready-made shapes called:
    a. AutoCharts
    b. AutoGraphics
    c. AutoShapes
    d. All of the above

15. After creating an AutoShape:
    a. You can change its size
    b. You can change the Fill and Line color
    c. You can move it over worksheet data
    d. All of the above

16. You can add text anywhere in the worksheet using a(n):
    a. Text box
    b. AutoBox
    c. Chart
    d. Worksheet Insert

17. Clip Art and Pictures can be added to a worksheet from:
    a. The ClipArt Gallery
    b. Pictures that you've scanned and saved in your computer
    c. Clip Gallery Live Web site
    d. All of the above

Student Workbook
Teach Yourself Excel 2000 VISUALLY

18. You can graphically display data that relates to specific geographic areas using the following feature:
    a. Data Map
    b. Text box
    c. Chart Wizard
    d. AutoShapes

19. To change the view of a chart to 3-D, you should:
    a. Click Chart and then select Type
    b. Click Chart and then select 3-D View
    c. Click Format and then select Chart
    d. Click Format and then deselect Default

20. You can quickly replot data to emphasize different information by:
    a. Double-clicking on the Chart tab and clicking the New Plot menu
    b. Selecting the Plot data by row or Plot data by column buttons on the Chart toolbar
    c. Choosing Format, Chart, and selecting Row or Column
    d. None of the above

MODULE 5
EXERCISES AND PROJECTS

Module 5 Fill-in-the-Blank Questions

Select the appropriate word from the list to fill in the blanks:

WORD LIST

AutoShapes
Chart Wizard
Clip Art Gallery
Data Series
Data Table
Delete
Handle
Insert Picture
Line, Area, and Column
Linked
One
Pattern
Preview
Row or Column
Scatter Chart
WordArt
Worksheet Data

1. Charts are _____ to worksheet data, so if you change the data, Excel automatically reflects the change in the chart.

2. Chart data can be plotted by _____.

3. To display the data used to create the chart, you can add a _____ to your chart.

4. Excel's _____ are ready-made shapes you can use to add graphics to a worksheet.

5. If you no longer want a graphic to appear in your worksheet, you can _____ the graphic.

6. To add a text effect to your worksheet, you can use the _____ feature.

7. The _____ is a library of clip art files you can insert into worksheets.

8. If you want to display your company's logo in a worksheet, use the _____ command.

9. If you are printing in black and white, you may want to change the _____ of a data series in a chart to make it easier to identify.

10. A pie chart can display only one _____.

11. You can print a chart on its own page or with the _____.

12. _____ charts are useful for displaying changes to values over time.

73

Student Workbook
Teach Yourself Excel 2000 VISUALLY

13. To see what a chart will look like when it's printed, you can _____ a chart.

14. To change the height of a chart, use the _____ on the top or bottom of the chart.

15. Use a _____ to compare pairs of values.

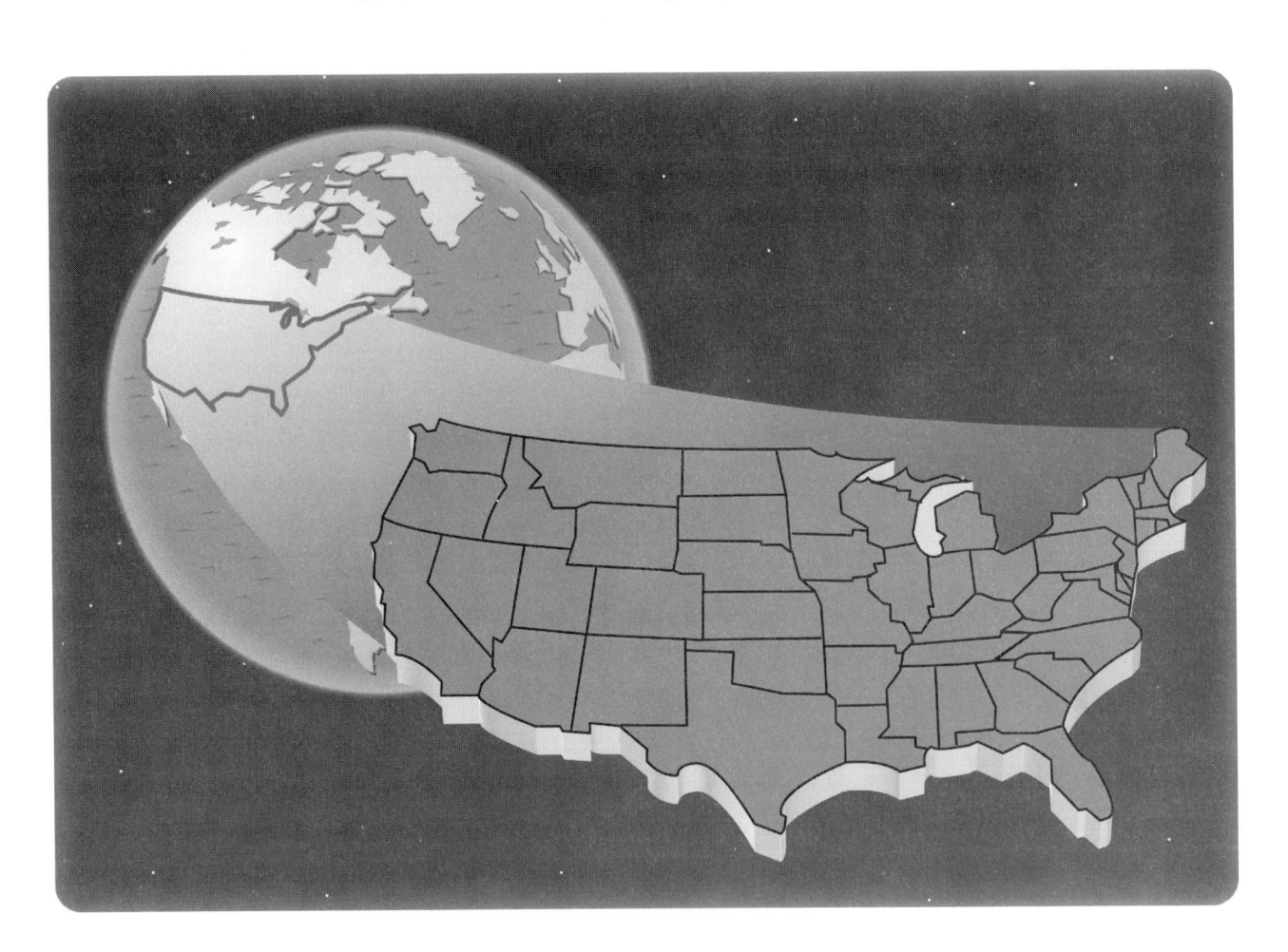

Module 5 Challenge Questions

Please use a sentence or a short paragraph to answer the following questions:

1. Describe, in order, the steps necessary to create a chart.

2. What are the differences between a Data Table and a Data Map?

3. List the five major components of most charts.

4. After creating a graphic object, you can change the height, width, or both of the graphic. Explain which handles you would use for each of these size changes.

5. List four of the standard chart types.

6. Explain how you would change the way Excel plots data.

7. You've created a chart on the same sheet as the worksheet data. Explain how you would print the chart with the worksheet data and print the chart by itself.

8. Describe the difference between elevation, rotation, and perspective in a 3-D chart view.

Student Workbook
Teach Yourself Excel 2000 VISUALLY

9. Explain how to update data in a Data Map.

_____

_____

10. If your company logo is stored in your computer, explain how you can add the logo to an Excel worksheet.

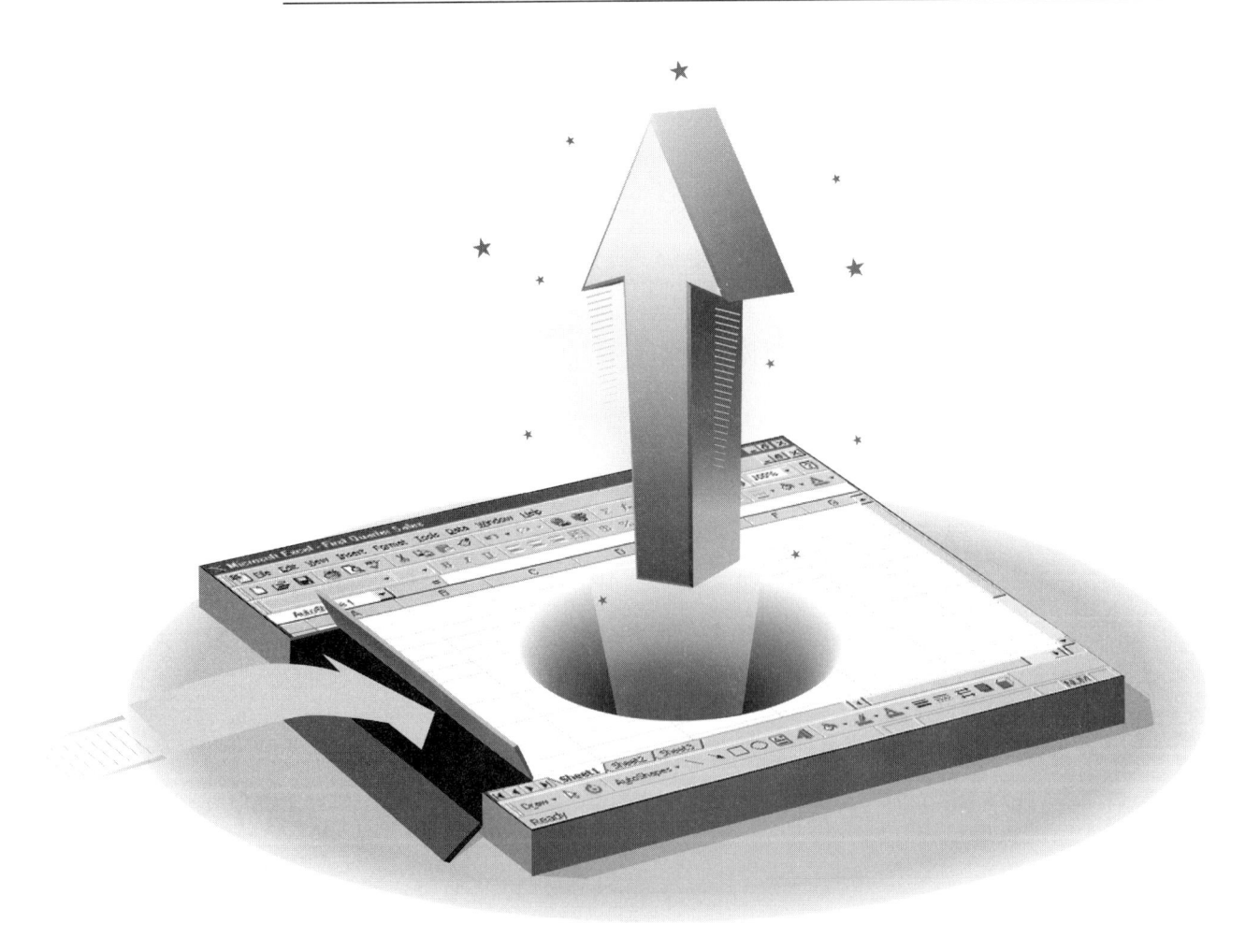

_____

_____

MODULE 5
EXERCISES AND PROJECTS

Project #1: Create a Chart

In this project, you can practice using the Chart Wizard to create a chart out of existing worksheet data.

Scenario:

As the CEO for National Enterprise Project Sales, you need to create a chart that displays Division sales from January to June. You want the chart to look similar to the following illustration.

National Enterprise Project Sales

	Jan	Feb	Mar	Apr	May	Jun
Division 1	$ 56,880.00	$ 57,332.00	$ 57,784.00	$ 58,236.00	$ 58,688.00	$ 59,140.00
Division 2	62,445.00	61,333.00	60,221.00	59,109.00	57,997.00	56,885.00
Division 3	$ 56,880.00	$ 57,332.00	$ 57,784.00	$ 58,236.00	$ 58,688.00	$ 59,140.00
Division 4	62,445.00	61,333.00	60,221.00	59,109.00	57,997.00	56,885.00
Division 5	$ 56,880.00	$ 57,332.00	$ 57,784.00	$ 58,236.00	$ 58,688.00	$ 59,140.00
Division 6	62,445.00	61,333.00	60,221.00	59,109.00	57,997.00	56,885.00
Division 7	$ 56,880.00	$ 57,332.00	$ 57,784.00	$ 58,236.00	$ 58,688.00	$ 59,140.00
	$ 414,855.00	$ 413,327.00	$ 411,799.00	$ 410,271.00	$ 408,743.00	$ 407,215.00

What you'll need:

A computer running Windows 95 or 98, and Microsoft Excel 2000
A printer, connected to the computer, with paper, online, and ready to print

What to do:

1. **Open the CHART.XLS file**
   a. Start Excel and click the Open button to display the Open dialog box.
   b. Double-click the CHART.XLS workbook.

2. **Enter data**
   a. Select cell A15 on Sheet1 tab, type your name, and press Enter twice on the keyboard.
   b. Type **Teach Yourself Excel 2000 VISUALLY** and press Enter twice on the keyboard.
   c. Type **Module 5 Project 1** in cell A19.

3. **Create a chart**
    a. Create a 3-D column chart as shown in the illustration at the beginning of this project.
    b. Add the appropriate titles as you proceed through the Chart Wizard.
    c. Elect to insert the chart on its own sheet.

4. **Save the workbook**
    a. Open the File menu and choose Save As.
    b. When the Save As dialog box opens, type **CHART2**, and then press Enter to save the workbook.

5. **Print the workbook**
    a. Make sure your printer is turned on, with paper loaded in the appropriate tray.
    b. Click the Print button on the Standard toolbar.

6. **Close Excel**
    a. Click the program window's Close button.

MODULE 5
EXERCISES AND PROJECTS

Project #2: Adding Graphics

In this project, you will practice using Excel's AutoShapes, text boxes, and other Drawing tools to create a quick and easy map.

Scenario:

You are having the annual employee picnic at the local park. Use Excel's Drawing tools to draw a map for the employees.

What to do:

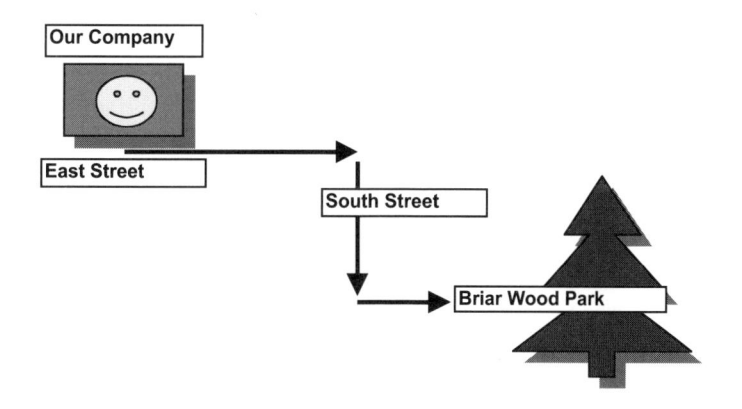

1. **Open the GRAPHICS.XLS file**
   a. Start Excel and click the Open button on the Standard toolbar.
   b. Double-click the GRAPHICS.XLS workbook file.

2. **Enter data**
   a. Select cell A18 on the Sheet1 tab, type your name, and press Enter twice on the keyboard.
   b. Type **Teach Yourself Excel 2000 VISUALLY** and press Enter twice on the keyboard.
   c. Type **Module 5 Project 2**.

3. **Display the Drawing toolbar**
   a. Open the View menu and choose Toolbars, Drawing.
   b. Using any drawing tool on the Drawing toolbar, create a map similar to the one shown in the illustration at the beginning of this project. Feel free to embellish your map as you wish, perhaps adding WordArt, or practice using the order commands to layer graphic objects on top of other objects. You can right-click any graphic object to display a shortcut menu with related commands.

4. **Save the workbook**
   a. Open the File menu and select Save As.
   b. When the Save As dialog box opens, type **GRAPHICS2**, and then press Enter to save the workbook.

5. **Print the workbook**
   a. Make sure your printer is turned on, with paper loaded in the appropriate tray.
   b. Click the Print button on the Standard toolbar.

6. **Close Excel**
   a. Click the Close button in the upper-right corner of the program window.

Taking It Even Further

Start the Excel program again, and then open the GRAPHICS2.XLS workbook. Use AutoShapes to add additional streets and landmarks. Use your imagination!

When you are finished with this project, be sure to save your work, and then exit Excel to prepare the computer for the next user and to free up resources in the computer.

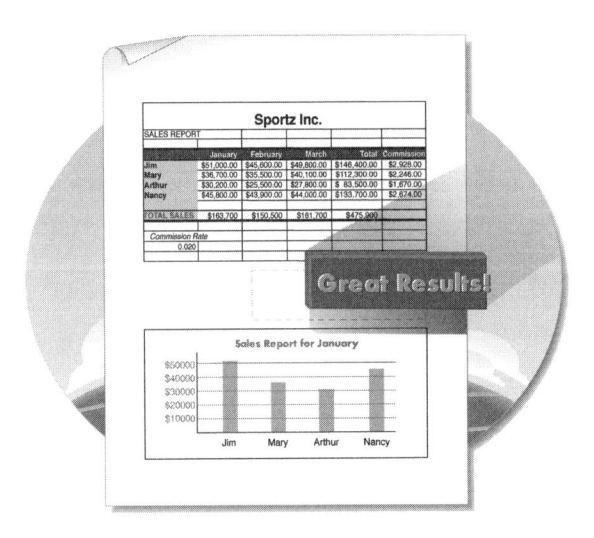

Module 6: Working with Macros, Lists, and Hyperlinks

Chapter Coverage

CHAPTER 11 MANAGE DATA IN A LIST
CHAPTER 12 TIME-SAVING FEATURES
CHAPTER 13 EXCEL AND THE INTERNET

Tests and Projects Included

Test Title	Chapter Reference
Module 6 Multiple Choice	11, 12, and 13
Module 6 Fill-in-the-Blank	11, 12, and 13
Module 6 Challenge Questions	11, 12, and 13

Project Title	Chapter Reference
Project 1 Creating a Macro	11, 12, and 13
Project 2 Applying a Custom AutoFilter	11, 12, and 13

Materials and Resources

The materials and resources required for successfully completing this module include:

- A computer running Microsoft Excel 2000
- Starter files for the projects
- A color monitor
- A printer, connected to the computer, loaded with paper, online, and ready to print
- At least 30 megabytes of available hard drive space

Student Workbook
Teach Yourself Excel 2000 VISUALLY

Module 6 Objectives

Upon completion of this module, you will be competent in the following areas:

Skill	Chapter
Creating a Database List	Chapter 11
Editing Records in a List	Chapter 11
Finding Records in a List	Chapter 11
Sorting Records in a List	Chapter 11
Filtering Records in a List	Chapter 11
Adding Subtotals to a List	Chapter 11
Creating a Custom Series	Chapter 12
Creating a Custom Toolbar	Chapter 12
Recording a Macro	Chapter 12
Running a Macro	Chapter 12
E-mailing a Worksheet	Chapter 13
Inserting a Hyperlink	Chapter 13
Saving Data as a Web Page	Chapter 13

Exercises and Projects

Module 6 Multiple Choice Questions
Please circle the letter in front of the correct response for each question.

1. You can begin creating your own customized toolbar using which command?
    a. Right-click over a toolbar and choose Customize
    b. Open the View menu and choose Toolbars, Customize
    c. Open the Tools menu and choose Customize
    d. All of the above

2. Macros are ideal for:
    a. Comparing various alternate values
    b. Tasks you perform repeatedly
    c. Creating a link between documents
    d. None of the above

3. When organizing a large amount of data, you would want to create a:
    a. Scenario
    b. List
    c. Macro
    d. Web page

4. Common database lists include:
    a. Mailing lists
    b. Phone directories
    c. Product lists
    d. All of the above

5. A column label:
    a. Describes the data in a column
    b. Is a group of related records
    c. Is displayed on the first row in a list
    d. Both a and c

Student Workbook
Teach Yourself Excel 2000 VISUALLY

6. What's the database term for a column label?
   a. Field
   b. Title
   c. Header
   d. All of the above

7. Sorting records by more than one column:
   a. Allows you to further organize the records in your list
   b. Is not possible in Excel
   c. Sorts your data, but only the first column will be alphabetical
   d. Messes up your rows and is not recommended

8. What is the purpose of filtering data in a list?
   a. Filtering lets you sort by more than one column
   b. Filtering displays only the first row of data
   c. Filtering lets you analyze your data by putting related records together and hiding the records you don't want to view
   d. Filtering lets you display only records that are greater than or less than the data you specify

9. You can quickly summarize data by:
   a. Using Filters
   b. Sorting the data in descending order
   c. Adding subtotals to your list
   d. None of the above

10. Which feature can you use to connect data in a workbook to another document or Web page?
   a. Hyperlink
   b. Filter
   c. Scenario
   d. List

11. How do you preview a workbook as a Web page?
   a. Use the Web Page Preview feature
   b. Open the Print dialog box
   c. Use the Print Preview window
   d. Display the Web toolbar

Module 6
Exercises and Projects

12. When editing records in a list:
    a. You can edit the record directly in the worksheet
    b. You can edit the records in the Data Form dialog box
    c. The record that needs to be edited will need to be located first
    d. All of the above

13. Which of the following can help you access information on the Internet from the Excel program window?
    a. Display the Web toolbar
    b. Use the Internet button on the Formatting toolbar
    c. Use the AutoFilter command
    d. Double-click the workbook's Title bar

14. To save a workbook as a Web page, use which of the following commands?
    a. Open the File menu and choose Internet
    b. Open the File menu and choose Save as Web Page
    c. Open the Format menu and choose HTML
    d. All of the above

15. What happens when you click the E-mail button on the Standard toolbar?
    a. A Web page opens onscreen
    b. Fields appear onscreen for entering e-mail addresses
    c. E-mail buttons appear for sending e-mail and attaching files
    d. Both b and c

16. How can you identify a hyperlink in a worksheet?
    a. The cell containing the hyperlink is outlined in red
    b. You cannot place hyperlinks in a worksheet
    c. The hyperlink appears underlined and in color
    d. The hyperlink appears italicized

17. What happens after subtotals are added to a list?
    a. They can be removed only by closing the file without saving changes
    b. They can be removed by selecting the Remove All button in the Subtotal dialog box
    c. You will not be able to filter worksheet data
    d. Excel will compare each record in the list

Student Workbook
Teach Yourself Excel 2000 VISUALLY

18. By which data types can you sort records in your list?
  a. Letter
  b. Number
  c. Date
  d. All of the above

19. Comparing data in a list can be accomplished by:
  a. Using a Custom AutoFilter
  b. Saving data as a Web page
  c. Using the Internet Assistant
  d. Using the Subtotal feature

20. What happens after a macro "runs" in Excel?
  a. The results cannot be undone
  b. The macro tasks will be performed as soon as you save the workbook
  c. You can click the Undo button if you don't like the results
  d. None of the above

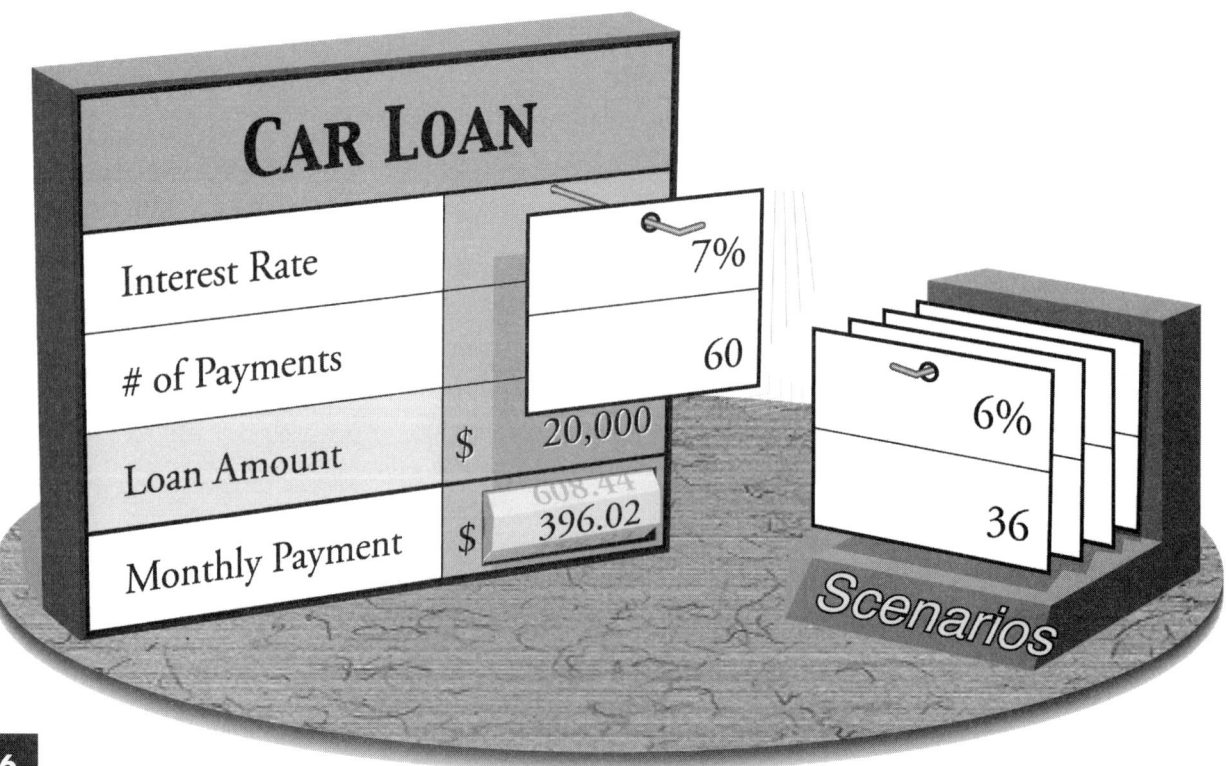

Module 6
EXERCISES AND PROJECTS

WORD LIST

AutoFilter
Column Label
Customize
Custom Series
Data Form
Field
Hyperlink
Keyboard Shortcut Key
List
Macro
Record
Save
Sorting
Subtotal
Web
Web Browser

Module 6 Fill-in-the-Blank Questions
Select the appropriate word from the list to fill in the blanks:

1. A _____ will automatically perform a series of commands that you record.

2. It's easy to customize toolbars in Excel using the _____ dialog box.

3. When entering repetitive data, such as a specialized list of names, turn the data into a _____.

4. A _____ is used to organize a large collection of data.

5. A _____ is a group of related data.

6. A _____ is one part of a record.

7. In Excel, a field appears as a _____ at the top of the database list.

8. You would use the _____ feature to analyze your data by placing related records together and hiding irrelevant records.

9. It is best to _____ your workbook before sorting records in case you do not get the desired results.

10. A quick way to run a macro is to assign it a _____.

11. _____ is a useful feature, especially if you frequently add new records to a list.

12. The _____ feature could be used to display employee names and sales and the grand total of all the sales.

87

Student Workbook
Teach Yourself Excel 2000 VISUALLY

13. A _____ can be created to take you from one document to another on your computer, network, corporate intranet, or the Internet.

14. Displaying the _____ toolbar allows you to access information on the Internet.

15. A Web page can be viewed in your _____.

Module 6 Challenge Questions

Please use a sentence or a short paragraph to answer the following questions:

1. Briefly describe how to create a custom data series.

2. Describe one way to tell Excel to insert a custom series you've previously stored.

3. List three places where a macro can be stored.

4. When you open a workbook containing macros, why does a dialog box appear? Describe the options that appear in the dialog box.

5. Describe what the first row of data in a database list contains.

6. Explain two methods for deleting a record in a list.

7. List and describe four common operators used in a database filter.

Student Workbook
Teach Yourself Excel 2000 VISUALLY

  8. Describe, in order, the steps necessary to start the AutoFilter feature.

  _____

  _____

  9. Explain the purpose of subtotals.

  _____

  _____

  10. Describe the purpose of Hyperlinks.

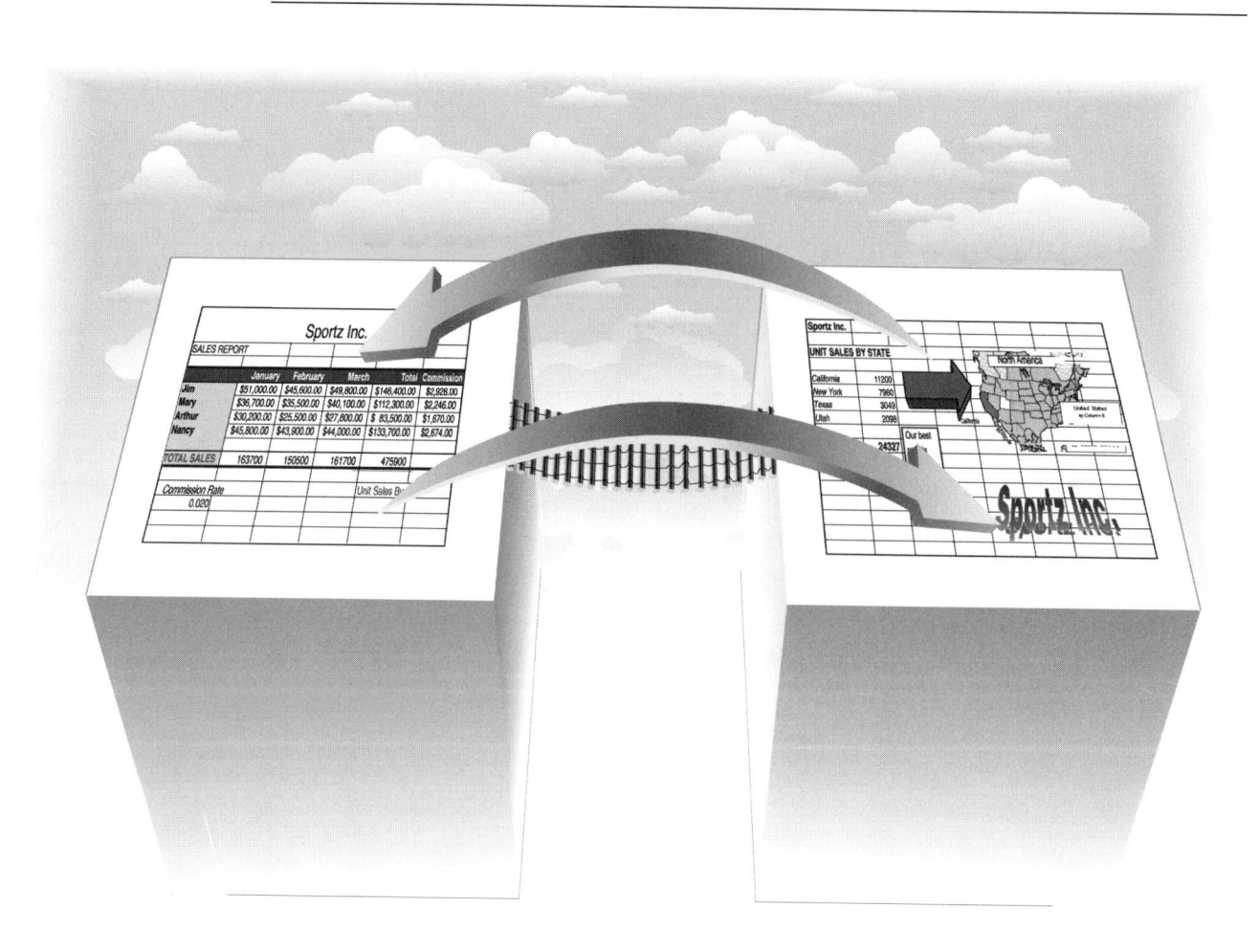

  _____

  _____

Project #1: Creating a Macro

Practice creating and running a macro in this project.

Scenario:

As the Sales Director for Petroleum Engineering National Products, you need to add additional titles to your worksheets. Because you will be adding these titles to numerous places throughout the workbook, you decide to create a macro for them.

What you'll need:

A computer running Windows 95 or 98 and Microsoft Excel 2000
A printer, connected to the computer, with paper, online, and ready to print

What to do:

1. **Open the MACRO.XLS workbook**
   a. Start Excel and display the Open dialog box.
   b. Open MACRO.XLS.

2. **Add data**
   a. Select cell D1 on Sheet1 tab and type your name and press Enter twice on the keyboard.
   b. Type **Teach Yourself Excel 2000 VISUALLY** and press Enter twice on the keyboard.
   c. Type **Module 6 Project 1**.

3. **Record a macro**
   a. Click Tools, select Macro, and choose Record New Macro.
   b. Enter **Titles** for the macro name and click OK.
   c. Type the following titles into cells A1, A2, and A3:
      Petroleum Engineering National Products
      Annual Sales
      Year Ending:
   d. Add boldface to each title.
   e. Make the text in cell A1 16 points, cell A2 14 points, and cell A3 12 points.
   f. Stop recording the macro.

4. Run the macro
   a. To add these titles to Sheet2, click the Sheet2 tab, and make sure cell A1 is selected.
   b. Click Tools, Macro, Macros.
   c. Select the Titles macro and click Run.

5. Save the workbook
   a. Select sheet 1, open the File menu, and select Save As.
   b. When the Save As dialog box opens, type **MACRO2**, and then press Enter to save the workbook.

6. Print the workbook
   a. Make sure your printer is turned on, with paper loaded in the appropriate tray.
   b. Click the Print button on the Standard toolbar.

7. Close Excel
   a. Click the program window's Close button.

Petroleum Engineering National Products				Student's Name	
Annual Sales					
Year Ending				Teach Yourself Excel 2000 Visually	
				Module 6 Project 1	
Costs					
Item	YEAR ENDING 1999		PROJECT COSTS FOR 2000		
Oil	$	210,000.00	$	220,000.00	
Gas	$	225,900.00	$	247,889.00	
Lignite	$	241,800.00	$	275,778.00	
Coal	$	257,700.00	$	303,667.00	
Total					
Income					
Item	YEAR ENDING 1999		PROJECT INCOME FOR 2000		
Oil	$	489,270.00	$	506,000.00	
Gas	$	504,660.00	$	523,459.00	
Lignite	$	520,050.00	$	540,918.00	
Coal	$	535,440.00	$	558,377.00	
Total					

MODULE 6
EXERCISES AND PROJECTS

Project #2: Applying a Custom AutoFilter

In this project, you practice using a Custom AutoFilter feature on a database list.

Scenario:

You are the Inventory Manager for your company. There is a sales presentation on Monday. You need to present a report that shows inventory items with a cost greater than $4.00. The following illustration shows the before and after results of this project.

Animal Supply Store Inventory			
Item No.	Description	Cost	Selling Price
P-CL10	Puppy Collar - 10"	$ 4.99	$ 7.50
P-SWSM	Puppy Sweater - Small	$ 6.65	$ 9.50
P-SWMD	Puppy Sweater - Medium	$ 8.65	$ 11.50
P-SWLG	Puppy Sweater - Large	$ 10.65	$ 13.50
K-KNSM	KittenNip - Small Bag	$ 4.50	$ 6.00
K-KNLG	KittenNip - Large Bag	$ 7.00	$ 8.50
Student's Name			
Teach Yourself Excel 2000 Visually			
Module 6 Project 2			

What to do:

1. **Open the LIST.XLS workbook file**
   a. Start Excel and display the Open dialog box.
   b. Open LIST.XLS.

2. **Enter data**
   a. Select cell A22 on the Sheet1 tab, type your name, and press Enter twice on the keyboard.
   b. Type **Teach Yourself Excel 2000 VISUALLY** and press Enter twice on the keyboard.
   c. Type **Module 6 Project 2**.

3. **Apply a Custom AutoFilter**
   a. Use the Custom AutoFilter feature to find all of the products in the list with a cost greater than $4.00.
   b. You should see six products displayed as a result of the filter.

4. **Save the workbook**
   a. Open the File menu and select Save As.
   b. When the Save As dialog box opens, type **LIST2**, and then press Enter to save the workbook.

5. **Print the workbook**
   a. Make sure your printer is turned on, with paper loaded in the appropriate tray.
   b. Click the Print button on the Standard toolbar.

6. **Close Excel**
   a. Click the program window's Close button.

Taking It Even Further

Start the Excel program again, and then open the LIST.XLS workbook. Remove the existing AutoFilter. Use AutoFilter to find Costs greater than $3.00 or Selling Price less than $10.00.

When you are finished with this project, be sure to save your work, and then exit Excel to prepare the computer for the next user and to free up resources in the computer.

Glossary

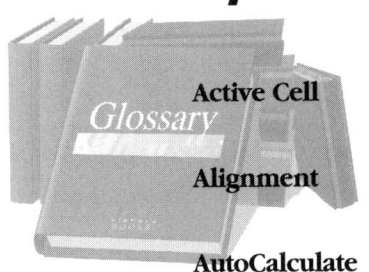

Active Cell	The cell that will be affected by the user's next actions. The active cell has a heavy border. Also called the selected cell.
Alignment	The position of data between the left and right edges and/or the top and bottom edges of the cell border.
AutoCalculate	An Excel feature through which common calculations are performed automatically on selected cells.
AutoCorrect	An Excel feature through which Excel automatically corrects common typing mistakes as you type.
AutoFilter	A list feature that allows you to display only the records containing data you want to view.
AutoFormat	An Excel feature through which predesigned formats can be applied to a worksheet.
AutoShape	An Excel feature through which a ready-made shape provided by Excel can be added to a worksheet.
Bold	A format that makes text appear thicker and darker.
Cell Reference	The name given to a cell, indicated by the column letter followed by the row number.
Chart	A graphical representation of worksheet data.
Chart Titles	Text that explains the chart, X-axis or Y-axis, and that appears within the chart.
Chart Type	The overall design of a chart, such as pie, column, line, bar, or area.
Click	Press the left mouse button and release.
Clipboard Toolbar	A floating toolbar that makes it easy to paste multiple items between worksheets and Office files.
Columns	A vertical line of cells in the worksheet. Columns are identified by letters.
Comment	Information or memos entered on a worksheet, marked by a red triangle in the upper-right corner of the cell.

Copy	Place a duplicate of a selected portion of a worksheet onto the Windows Clipboard, leaving the selected portion of the document untouched.
Cut	Delete a selected portion of a worksheet and place it on the Windows Clipboard.
Data Map	A display of geographic information in a worksheet in a graphical (visual) format.
Delete	Remove a selected portion of a worksheet.
Double-Click	Place the mouse pointer on an item and quickly press the left mouse button twice.
Edit	Change existing information.
Filter	Display specific records in a data list. For example, you may want to filter a data list to find only those customers living in the state of Texas.
Find	Locate a word or a number in the current worksheet.
Footer	Information that appears at the bottom of the printed page of your worksheet. This information can include the page number, name of the preparer, and so on.
Format	Change the appearance of text or data. This may include such formatting as bold, italic, font size, currency format, and so on.
Freeze	Fix the position of columns and/or rows so they do not scroll when the rest of the worksheet scrolls. This is generally used to ensure that column or row headings are always visible.
Function	A small program that performs an operation on data and returns a single value. Multiple functions can be combined within formulas. For example, =SUM(A5..A10) would add the values in cells A5, A6, A7, A8, A9, and A10 and display the result in the cell in which the formula was defined.
Graphic Objects	Shapes and images you can produce on a worksheet.
Header	Information printed at the top of each page of a printed report.
Hyperlink	A shortcut to a document on your computer, across networks, or on the Internet.
Indent	Move data from the left edge of the cell.

GLOSSARY

Insert	Add new data in the middle of existing data by inserting cells, columns, or rows.
Italic	A text format that produces slanted type.
Landscape	Paper that is wider than it is tall, such as 11" x 8 1/2".
Legend	Chart information that helps identify the chart data.
List	A group of related data organized in a useful manner. A list is made up of records that are further divided into fields.
Macro	A series of frequently used tasks that are recorded and stored under a single command. Excel plays the macro back and performs the recorded tasks.
Margin	The amount of space between worksheet contents and the edge of the paper.
Maximize Button	A control used to change the size of a window. Click it to enlarge a window to fill the screen. If the window already fills the screen, the Maximize button is replaced by the Restore button. Clicking the Restore button returns the window to its previous size.
Minimize Button	A control used to reduce the size of a window. Click it to reduce a window to a button at the bottom of the program window. Clicking the Restore button returns the window to its previous size.
Mouse	A handheld device that lets you select and move items on your screen.
Office Assistant	An Excel feature that helps you locate information on how to perform a task.
Open	The command that lets you view a previously saved document.
Operator	A symbol that indicates the type of operation a formula is to perform.
Orientation	Determines the way a sheet prints. Portrait refers to printing on paper taller than it is wide. Landscape refers to printing on paper wider than it is tall.
Page Break Preview	Displays the page breaks in a worksheet.
Portrait	Paper that is taller than it is wide, such as 8 1/2" by 11".
Print Preview	The Excel feature that lets you see on your screen how the worksheet will look when it's printed.
Protect	The Excel feature that prevents other people from opening or making changes to a workbook by protecting it with a password.

Replace	Exchange the data in a cell with new data. To replace data in a cell, click in the cell, type the new data, and press Enter.
Rotate	The Excel feature that lets you change the angle of text or numbers in a cell.
Row	A horizontal line of cells. Rows are indicated by numbers.
Save	Store a workbook on a disk for future use.
Save As	Store a copy of a previously saved workbook under a different name.
Scenario	The Excel feature that lets you view various results, such as a change to net income, when data within a worksheet is changed.
Scroll	Bring other parts of the screen into view.
Scroll Bar	The bar containing scroll arrows and the scroll box that allows you to view unseen parts of your worksheet onscreen.
Scroll Box	On a scroll bar, a box that you drag to bring other parts of the screen into view.
Select	Choose a portion of a worksheet to work with. Selected cells are surrounded by a heavy border. Selected graphics and charts have handles (small squares) along their edges.
Series	A collection of text or numbers that form a logical progression. An example of a text series would be January, February, March, and so on. An example of a number series would be 5, 10, 15, 20, 25.
Sort	Rearrange the order of records in a list.
Split	Segment a worksheet into separate sections so you can view more than one part of the worksheet at one time.
Subtotal	The sum of a group of related values in a list, such as sales per quarter or expenses per month.
Toolbar	Bar with a group of related tools that you can click to perform specific tasks.
Underline	A line under text or numbers.
Web	The World Wide Web—a part of the Internet—where you can access a wide variety of information using a computer, an Internet Service Provider, and a Web browser.
Web Browser	Software that displays Web pages that are downloaded to your computer from the Internet.

GLOSSARY

Web Page	A page of interest that has been placed on the Internet.
Workbook	An Excel file that contains worksheets. You keep related information together in a workbook.
Worksheet	The grid-like structure in which you enter spreadsheet data. It consists of a collection of columns and rows.
Wrap Text	The Excel feature that allows Excel to perform word wrap, where entire words are moved to a new line when they will not fit on the line above.
X-Axis	Typically the horizontal axis on a chart. This axis usually displays categories of data.
Y-Axis	Typically the vertical axis on a chart. This axis usually displays numeric data.
Zoom	Increase or decrease the magnification of a window and its contents on a computer screen.

Student Workbook
Teach Yourself Excel 2000 VISUALLY

Notes

Notes

Notes

my2cents.idgbooks.com

Register This Book — And Win!

Visit **http://my2cents.idgbooks.com** to register this book and we'll automatically enter you in our fantastic monthly prize giveaway. It's also your opportunity to give us feedback: Let us know what you thought of this book and how you would like to see other topics covered.

Discover IDG Books Online!

The IDG Books Online Web site is your online resource for tackling technology — at home and at the office. Frequently updated, the IDG Books Online Web site features exclusive software, insider information, online books, and live events!

10 Productive & Career-Enhancing Things You Can Do at www.idgbooks.com

- Nab source code for your own programming projects.
- Download software.
- Read Web exclusives: special articles and book excerpts by IDG Books Worldwide authors.
- Take advantage of resources to help you advance your career as a Novell or Microsoft professional.
- Buy IDG Books Worldwide titles or find a convenient bookstore that carries them.
- Register your book and win a prize.
- Chat live online with authors.
- Sign up for regular e-mail updates about our latest books.
- Suggest a book you'd like to read or write.
- Give us your 2¢ about our books and about our Web site.

You say you're not on the Web yet? It's easy to get started with IDG Books' *Discover the Internet,* available at local retailers everywhere.